THIS BO 〔barcode〕
YO
PRO〕
TEACH YOU . . .

Colleges exist to serve you, not the other way around.

You don't have to finish college in four years.

No one does all the work in every class.

Do not take a class that starts before 10 A.M. unless you know you can make it without losing sleep.

Many classes are boring—the trick is not to settle for boring teachers.

Employers normally care very little about your college grades, and rarely ask to see them.

There are exceptions to every college rule and regulation.

Almost nothing that happens in college is a genuine disaster or a permanent liability.

. . . AND MUCH, MUCH
MORE—IN THIS
LIFESAVING GUIDE TO
COLLEGE SURVIVAL
IN THE '80S

SCOTT EDELSTEIN

College:
A User's Manual

**All the Important Things
No One Else Will Tell You
About College and College Life**

BANTAM BOOKS

TORONTO • NEW YORK • LONDON • SYDNEY • AUCKLAND

COLLEGE: A USER'S MANUAL
A Bantam Book / September 1985

Book design by Nicola Mazzella

Library of Congress Cataloging-in-Publication Data

Edelstein, Scott.
  College, a user's manual.

  1. College student orientation—United States—Handbooks, manuals, etc. I. Title.
LB2343.32.E34 1985   378'.198'0973   85-47616
ISBN 0-553-34194-4 (pbk.)

Published simultaneously in the United States and Canada

Bantam Books are published by Bantam Books, Inc. Its trademark, consisting of the words "Bantam Books" and the portrayal of a rooster, is Registered in U.S. Patent and Trademark Office and in other countries. Marca Registrada. Bantam Books, Inc., 666 Fifth Avenue, New York, New York 10103.

PRINTED IN THE UNITED STATES OF AMERICA

FG   0 9 8 7 6 5 4 3 2 1

For my parents,
Joe and Estelle

CONTENTS

Why You Need This Book

If you are a college student, or if you are planning to be one, you have already been given a great many tips by teachers, advisers, guidance counselors, and books. A lot of this information is valuable and useful.

But the most important information—the information that is crucial to your happiness and success in college—usually doesn't get passed on by administrators, teachers, parents, counselors, catalogs and bulletins, or college guides. And, until now, most of these important tips, shortcuts, and livesaving maneuvers had to be learned the hard way—through your own trial and error, your own success and failure, and your own painful experiences.

College: A User's Manual contains just this vital information, which will help make your years in college happier and more successful ones.

This book isn't only for college freshmen and high school seniors. It's got tips, advice, and useful information for all students—including juniors, seniors, and graduate students. It can also be a big help to non-traditional students: part-timers, students over the age of 30, extension students, people with full-time jobs, foreign students, and non-degree students. Much of this information probably will be new to you, even if you have been in college for a while. Some of it may be surprising. And almost all of it will turn out to be very useful.

As a college teacher and adviser for the past seven years, I've often been surprised at all the important information and advice that teachers, advisers, administrators, and parents never pass on to students. And I've been dismayed and shocked at the useless, sometimes harmful, and sometimes ridiculous advice that these people give to students.

This book is a sane and practical guide to help you fill in these gaps and cut through the misinformation so that you can get through college with a minimum of confusion and pain.

Much of this information is the result of my own experience as a college teacher; a lot of it I learned the hard way, on my own, as a student. Some of it has come to me from some of my saner and wiser colleagues, both teachers and administrators. And some was passed on to me when I was a student by other students with intelligence and savvy.

This book is broken down into twelve chapters, with each chapter focusing on a different aspect of college life. Each chapter presents a number of key points of information, and after each point is a detailed explanation.

You can read this book in two ways. You can read any pertinent chapter, or any pertinent section within a chapter. Or, if you are lazy, pressed for time, or willing to take my wisdom on faith, you can just read the headings for each section. The headings will give you a good, clear idea of the real options, shortcuts, pitfalls, potential problems, and possible solutions that exist for you as a student. However, in some cases you will need to read the explanation that follows to learn how to put the information in the heading into action.

I expect that there will be future editions of this book. If there are any important tips that you think your fellow students should know, please write to me in care of this publisher. Worthwhile information will be duly added in the next edition, along with my grateful acknowledgment.

Scott Edelstein
Kent, Ohio

CHAPTER 1

What You Should Know from the Start

College is not for everybody.

Nor does everybody need it. It is very possible to get a good job, to have a successful and rewarding career, and to live a happy life without a college degree, or without any college at all. There are, after all, plenty of other options: work, vocational or technical school, apprenticeship, and individual entrepreneurship.

On the other hand, college *can* do a great many things for many people in terms of education, career preparation, and training, in addition to helping them to grow as human beings.

There are many good reasons for going to college. It doesn't matter whether your main interest is career preparation, your own personal growth, intellectual and emotional fulfillment, simple curiosity, or the desire to have a good time. If you want to go to college, whatever the reason, go. But if college *doesn't* interest you, do something else.

Whatever you decide, remember that that decision is not irrevocable. If you decide to go to college, you will always have the options of dropping out, transferring, and taking some time off. If you decide not to go to college now, you can always go sometime in the future.

A bachelor's degree does not mean as much as it used to; however, it still means a great deal.

Thirty years ago, a bachelor's degree was a sign of special effort and achievement, and that degree was held in high esteem.

Today, bachelor's degrees are far more common. Most high school graduates go on to earn at least some college credits, and today no one thinks of a bachelor's degree as something special.

However, a bachelor's degree can still make a big difference in your employability. It is an important qualification for a great many white-collar jobs. (See chapter 8 for more information on this subject.)

And, despite the reduced prestige of a degree, college still can do a great deal to help you become an educated, thinking, happy, and wise human being.

There is nothing wrong with taking a year off between high school and college to work, travel, or pursue a special interest. Taking this time off cannot harm you, and it can be enormously rewarding.

This year off can be one of tremendous growth, adventure, and fun. It can also teach you about the real world—especially the working world—and how it functions. I highly recommend this year off for anyone wary of going straight from high school into college. But I do not recommend it for everyone. If you want to go straight from high school to college, by all means do. After all, college can be a time of tremendous growth, adventure, and fun, too.

No employer, graduate school, or professional school will penalize you or look down on you in any way for having taken this time off.

If you wish, you can arrange your enrollment in college before your year off begins. Most colleges will allow you to opt for what is called *deferred admission*. This means that you agree to attend not in the coming fall or coming term, but at some later agreed-upon date. The college, in turn, agrees to enroll you automatically at that time. Most students apply for deferred admission during their senior year of high school, just like regular college applicants. At most schools, you also have the option of submitting a regular application for admission, then, once you are accepted, arranging to enroll on a deferred basis.

For more information on this topic, see the section entitled "Taking Time Off" in Chapter 9.

Carefully choose the college you will attend. Do not pick a school just because your friends are going there, or because your parents recommended or attended it.

When you choose to enroll at a college, you are agreeing to abide by its rules and policies, academic and otherwise, and you are subjecting yourself to its teachers, courses, and academic programs. You are also throwing yourself into that college's social life, and its physical and emotional environment. All of these can differ tremendously from school to school.

If your parents both went to Colby College, but you feel that Ohio State better suits you and your interests, go to Ohio State. Select a school that suits your own personality, needs, desires, goals, and interests. Choose carefully—it can make the difference between happiness and misery, and between academic success and academic failure.

If possible, before you apply, but always before you enroll, visit the colleges you are thinking of attending.

College catalogs and brochures, and the spiels of admissions representatives, cannot give you a complete or clear picture of what a college is really like. The only way to get a true feel for a college is to be there. A visit all but eliminates the possibility of disappointment when a school turns out to be vastly different from how it seemed on paper.

When visiting, stay in a dorm room so you can get a good feel for everyday on-campus life. Most colleges can arrange this for you through their admissions offices.

One of the best ways to learn about a school is to ask students. Pick a few students who look friendly and approachable and who seem like they might have sensibilities similar to your own. Introduce yourself politely, explain that you're thinking of attending their college, and ask questions.

Talking to teachers is also a good idea. Most teachers will be happy to talk to you for a few minutes. Pick instructors who sound interesting, or whose course offerings look intriguing, or who have been recommended to you by students, or who might end up being your advisers or instructors. Spend a few minutes chatting with them during their office hours. Department offices should have on file the office numbers, phone numbers, and office hours of every instructor within that department.

Some questions you might want to ask teachers and students are:

■ What are the strengths of this school—academically, socially, and administratively?

■ What are some of the weaknesses of this school—academically, socially, and administratively?

■ What are the strengths and weaknesses of the particular department you teach or major in?

■ What are some of your own interests, both academic and non-academic?

■ Do you like it here? Why? Why not?

Don't take the opinions of students or teachers as gospel, of course. You must judge for yourself how well suited a school is for you. But also use your intuition and feelings.

Try to sit in on some classes. Get a copy of the current class schedule from the registrar and pick out courses or teachers that sound interesting. Ask each teacher if you can sit in quietly on one of his or her classes. Some may refuse, which is their right, but most probably will be happy to oblige.

When you do sit in on a class, sit in the rear of the classroom; quietly observe but do not participate unless the instructor specifically asks you to do so.

If you wish to sit in on a teacher's class, it is best to learn his or her office hours and to call or visit the teacher in his or her office to ask if you can observe the class. This also gives you the chance to talk with him or her privately for a few minutes. If this is not possible, show up in the classroom a few minutes before class begins to make your request.

Attend one or two of the school's social events if possible.

Spend some time at the student union and other public areas and soak up the atmosphere.

Take a guided tour of the school. Almost every school offers such tours. Tours may be offered only on certain days, however, so it is preferable to arrange a tour in advance through the admissions office.

Do not choose a college merely because it is prestigious.

A great many high school seniors think that it is important to go to a school with a good reputation. In general, however, a college's reputation makes little difference.

The quality of instruction at any institution, or in any particular program, is exactly as good, or as poor, as each individual teacher. This means that at every college, the quality of teaching runs the entire range from pathetic to sensational. There are some terrific teachers at every community college and commuter school, and there are some terrible ones at Harvard. The trick is to find the good teachers wherever you are. The general *level* at which courses are taught does vary from school to school, the better schools offering more demanding courses, but the quality of the teaching is variable everywhere.

If you can't wait to get out of high school, it is sometimes possible to go directly to college after your junior year.

Many colleges, especially the better ones, admit a small group of these students each year. If you are accepted, you will not receive a high school diploma, but you *will* be granted regular freshman status. Sometimes admission in the middle of your senior year can also be arranged.

Normally this option is available only to students with high intelligence, promise, potential, excellent SAT or ACT scores, or particular artistic or academic achievement. Check with the admissions office of the school in question for policies and application procedures.

There are seven other ways to get into college without a high school diploma.

1. Pass the GED test. Passing this test certifies that you know everything a high school graduate should. This is equivalent to a high school diploma, and most colleges will accept a passing score on the GED exam in lieu of a diploma. Check with the counseling office in your local high school, or with the college admissions office or testing office for more information.

2. Most extension, community education, continuing education, weekend, and evening college programs are open to everyone, regardless of their educational background. You must enroll in these programs as a non-degree student in most cases. However, after a year or two, you can apply to a degree program at that or another college. If you have done C-level work or better, you will have evidence that you can handle college-level work, and there is a fair to good chance that you will be admitted to that degree program, despite your lack of a high school diploma.

3. Many community colleges offer open enrollment to all interested people over a certain age, usually over 17. You can enroll in an associate degree program regardless of your educational background, or lack of it. Once you've completed a year or more of satisfactory work at the community college, you can very likely transfer to a four-year school. Or you can complete your associate degree at the community college.

4. Some large universities, particularly state universities, offer a program very similar to the one described above. Such a program is often called the Community College or the General College. Check with the school's registrar for details.

5. Some schools will allow you to enroll in the regular day school as a non-degree student, even if you lack a high school diploma. Once you have completed 30 or more credits of satisfactory work, you can apply to a degree program, and there is a good chance that you will be admitted. Check with the registrar for details.

6. Many schools, especially the large state universities, offer special programs for minorities and "educationally disadvantaged" students. They are generally open only to blacks, Hispanics, Native Americans, Eskimos, certain foreign students, and/or students whose native tongue is not English. Some of these programs are also open to students who do not have high school diplomas. Check with the registrar for details.

7. If you are especially bright, or if you have special talents or achievements in one particular area, some colleges will be willing to waive the high school diploma requirement. I know several unusually intelligent and creative people who found high school not merely tedious but insufferable. They dropped out after the ninth or tenth grade with abominable academic records. But when they applied to college a few years later, with evidence of their particular skills and achievements, they were admitted to top schools. You might give this option a shot. It is particularly viable for talented people in the arts who are applying to arts schools or to liberal arts colleges with strong artistic bents. (Note: the better a school is academically, the more likely it is, in general, to accept you on such a basis.)

Please note that if you enroll in any school or program as a non-degree student, you will not qualify for some forms of financial aid.

Never write off a college because you feel you can't afford it.

Most colleges are committed to providing financial aid to students who genuinely need it, no matter how great their need. This is true even of the most expensive schools. In fact, some of the highest-priced schools also have the most money available for financial aid.

Of course, financial aid comes from the federal and state governments and from private scholarship funds, as well as from the individual colleges. But among the many different financial aid options, there is a pretty good chance that a school, even a very expensive one, can put together an aid package that will make that school affordable for you.

If you are turned down by the college of your choice, there may still be ways to get in.

1. If the school has an extension, community education, continuing education, weekend, or evening program, chances are that the courses in that program are open to all interested students, even those who have been refused admission to the regular degree program. Enroll as a non-degree student, and after two or more terms, if you have done fairly well, then there is a good chance that if you apply for admission to the degree program, you'll get in.

2. Check with the school's registrar to see if there is an "open enrollment" division or program within that school.

3. Ask if you can enroll in the regular college program as a non-degree student.

4. Enroll elsewhere and work hard. Next year reapply to the college of your choice as a transfer student. If your grades are good, you will probably be admitted.

5. If you are a minority or foreign student, you may be able to get admitted under one of the special programs described earlier in this chapter. Check with the registrar.

If you do enroll as a non-degree student, you will not qualify for some forms of financial aid.

Don't overlook alternative and experimental colleges.

With a few exceptions, colleges that initiated unusual or innovative academic programs in the 1960s and 1970s have now become respectable and recognized, while remaining innovative. Most are financially and organizationally quite stable. Most are accredited, and most award degrees worth as much or more to employers and graduate and professional schools as degrees from traditional schools.

Most of these schools allow and expect students to design their own personal academic programs, and most offer a high degree of academic self-direction and freedom, as well as plenty of social freedom. A few, however, have unusual programs that are innovative in many ways but that are *more* restrictive than the academic programs in traditional schools.

Some alternative college programs allow you to do most or all of your work off-campus. Some require students to attend short-term residencies lasting a week or two, followed by six-month periods of supervised independent study. A very few schools offer programs based *entirely* on supervised independent study.

If traditional schools do not interest you; or if you want the freedom to choose your own direction and design your own program; or if your academic interests are unusual, then you should look seriously into some of these schools.

The best guide to experimental and alternative colleges is *How to Get the Degree You Want: Bear's Guide to Nontraditional College Degrees* by John Bear, Ph.D. (Berkeley, Calif.: Ten Speed Press, 1982). This book describes and evaluates each college and its programs.

CHAPTER 2

Getting a Good Start

It is almost impossible to be a full-time student and work more than five to ten hours per week. Likewise, it is almost impossible to work full-time and take more than one 3- or 4-credit course per term.

Keep these limits very much in mind. There are only so many hours in the day. There is no point in committing yourself to more than you can genuinely handle. If you do, you will either find yourself going crazy, or cutting a person or activity out of your life, whether you like it or not. So limit your commitments in advance.

If you have children, a spouse, a boyfriend or girlfriend, or some combination thereof, remember that each of them will demand (and deserve) some of your time. Be sure to allow for these people in your schedule.

Obviously, the limits I've given above are not absolutes. Your actual limits depend on the difficulty of the courses you are taking; the amount of energy and thought your job requires, and the amount of stress it produces; and your own personal rhythms, stamina, and needs. Still, time has a way of always being scarcer than we expect, no matter how carefully we plan. So let me make the following recommendations:

■ If you must work and go to school, consider doing both part-time. But remember that part-time status as a student will reduce your eligibility for certain kinds of financial aid.

■ If you are working full-time, perhaps you can temporarily reduce your work week—say, from forty hours to thirty-five.

■ If you must be a full-time student, take the minimum number of credits permitted for full-time status. It is usually twelve per term.

■ If you are a full-time student, try to take at least one or two classes per term that are fairly easy or fun, or at least not time-consuming. (This is good advice even for students who are not working.)

Don't overload your schedule, academically or otherwise.

Even if you are not holding down a paying job, it is all too easy to overcommit yourself, what with school, hobbies, family, friends, lovers, daily chores, minor emergencies, religious activities, and the thousand other things that make up daily life. So be very careful and conscious of how much time you actually have and what you genuinely are able to do, and want to do, with that time.

Take it easy during your first year of college. Don't take on too many responsibilities, especially academic ones.

No one—least of all your teachers and your adviser—expects you to work yourself to death as a freshman. You are, after all, making a great many intellectual and emotional transitions, and you are making the very large change from adolescence to adulthood. This change cannot be made overnight—it takes time, learning, mistakes, and pain. So you are entitled to some slack. Most schools are going to allow you some—so be sure to allow *yourself* some.

At least one or two of your classes should be fun, or easy, or both. And if you are a full-time student, I recommend taking the minimum number of credits permitted for full-time status, at least during your first term. You can always increase your course load next term or next year if you want.

In short, go ahead and have a good time. Relax. Take your classes seriously, of course, but don't tell yourself, "I'm an adult now, so I have to be serious and responsible." No adult with a whole brain and a whole heart tries to be "serious and responsible" all the time. In fact, an important part of maturity is knowing when to be serious and responsible and when to be otherwise.

Learning to write well should be one of your very first and most important goals as a college student.

Good writing is the basis of success in many college classes. There is a strong correlation between the quality of a student's writing and his or her grades.

The ability to write well is also a skill that will prove extremely useful later in many jobs.

Chapter 6 will provide lots of useful writing tips.

Typing is a very valuable skill for college students. If you don't know how to type, it is a good idea to learn.

Typing is much faster than writing by hand, and typed papers almost always look better than handwritten ones. Certainly typed papers are easier on teachers' weary eyes and brains. A substantial percentage of teachers *require* all papers to be typewritten, which means that if you learn how to type, you will also save the cost of hiring a typist.

Typing is not difficult to learn, and once you learn, it will make a great many things easier. Business letters, resumes, and even personal letters will be quick, easy, and convenient to write. Many students find that they actually compose better papers on a typewriter or computer than they do in longhand. Personally, I do *all* my writing, except grocery lists, on a typewriter.

Typing will also pay off after you graduate and join the working world. Typing is a skill needed for many jobs— secretarial work, any job that includes writing, and so on. And it is very useful even for those jobs which do not absolutely demand it.

Remember, too, that computers are making their way deeper and deeper into all aspects of our lives. And to use a computer well you need to know how to type.

A good many colleges offer classes in typing for credit. If you can't already type, take a typing class. This will teach you this extremely valuable skill while earning you college credit at the same time.

Don't be afraid of computers.

First off, you should know that some schools do require computer literacy (the ability to use computers and/or the knowledge of one basic computer language) for graduation with a bachelor's degree. Others require every student to take a one- or two-semester course in computer usage. A few require you to actually buy a personal computer when you first enroll; and a very few will require computer literacy for admission as a freshman. Some colleges have one of these requirements only in certain schools and programs. If you are an absolute and incurable computerphobe, you may want to avoid such schools and programs. Check with your registrar to see whether a computer course or computer literacy will be required.

Probably one student out of three or four is not only unable to use a computer, but quite sure that he or she will never be able to use them. I was such a student myself. I felt uncomfortable around computers and, at first, was unable to do anything but turn on a terminal without feeling angry, intimidated, and anxious.

However, there is hope for students who feel the way I used to. First, there are a couple of books which can help: *Computer Wimp* by John Bear (Ten Speed Press) and *The Beginner's Guide to Computers* by Robin Bradbeer, Peter DeBono, and Peter Laurie (Addison-Wesley). Second, while computers are a big challenge (and a bigger pain) to learn to use at first, after five to ten hours of practice, things will suddenly start to become easy and familiar, at least for most students. After five to ten more hours of practice, the last of your computer fears will almost certainly vanish. You won't be an expert yet, of course, but you will no longer think of computers as mean, ugly, and intimidating.

College is a great place to try some things that are new to you, some things that are different, some things that are difficult, and even some things that are threatening.

Go ahead and try them. One of the best things about college is that no matter what you try, you have very little to lose. Probably the worst that can happen emotionally is that you feel a little foolish, or that you discover some of your own weaknesses or limitations. But this isn't really so bad at all. I was class dunce in a couple of my college courses (Spanish I and Trampoline), and I still had fun in both, and passed both, too.

And the worst that can happen academically is that you do poorly in certain classes—but there are ways to cut this risk down to virtually zero, as you will learn in future chapters.

Colleges exist to serve you, not the other way around.

Although the primary responsibility and role of a college is to serve its students, a lot of students, parents, teachers, and administrators seem to have forgotten this.

You do not have to finish college in four years.

Education is not a race to the finish line, nor should it be a rat race of full-time study for four straight years. You are not going to fall behind or get left in the dust if you go slower; there will still be plenty of good jobs and graduate schools a year or two later. Employers, graduate and professional school admissions committees, and scholarship and fellowship selection committees do not look down on part-time students, or on students who have taken time off or dropped out and then returned to school later, or on students who have taken light course loads on a regular basis.

Some ways to save money on textbooks:

■ Check the books out of your college library. This may seem like preposterously elementary advice, but I have found that students almost *never* go to the library for a book they will need for a class. Even if a book costs forty dollars, students will plunk down the forty dollars rather than get the book on loan, free. And if a book you need is not available in your college's library, you can still get it through that library on interlibrary loan. See details below.

■ If your college library doesn't have a book you're looking for, check the local public libraries.

■ If there are other colleges in your area, check their libraries too. You can usually arrange borrowing privileges at any library in your area at no charge.

■ Check used-book stores, especially those near campus and those near other colleges in your area.

■ Check your college bookstore. A number of these bookstores carry used texts at reduced prices.

■ Don't overlook used-book sales sponsored by your school or student union. Such sales usually are held at the beginning of each term.

■ Teachers will not always assign the cheapest edition of a particular book. Check *Books in Print* in your library to find out what editions of each title are available and what each edition costs. If a cheaper edition is available, check with your instructor before buying it. Occasionally an instructor will want students to use a particular edition or translation.

You can get virtually any book in the world, no matter how old or obscure, through interlibrary loan at your college library or any public library.

With the advent of computerized cataloguing, every library in the country has access to the list of titles available in almost every other library in the country. Out of this has grown an extremely thorough and efficient (though not always quick) interlibrary loan system.

If your college library does not have a particular book, ask a librarian to get it for you through interlibrary loan.

Interlibrary loan rarely fails to locate a book. However, there may be a time lag in getting the book to you. Sometimes a book arrives in a day or two; two weeks is an average time; and six to eight weeks is not unheard of.

Normally there is no charge, or a charge of a dollar per request, for interlibrary loan items. Generally a book on interlibrary loan may be checked out for one month.

Magazine and newspaper articles are also available via interlibrary loan. Records, films, microfilms, filmstrips, and other library items are sometimes, though not always, available.

What to do if your college bookstore is sold out of a particular book you need for a class:

■ First, check the general books area of the bookstore. Often all the copies of a book will have been sold from the textbook section, but a few copies will be for sale as a general-interest book. This is especially true of books for humanities courses.

■ Ask a bookstore employee if the book you want is available elsewhere in the store. Perhaps copies of the book arrived earlier in the day but have not yet been put on the shelves. Or perhaps copies of the book are in the psychology section and you had only checked the sociology and women's studies sections.

■ Explain to your instructor that the bookstore is out of copies of the book. Ask politely if he or she will loan you a copy until you can find one elsewhere. Most teachers have more than one copy of many texts, and usually they are happy to loan out their extras to students who need them. Occasionally a teacher may even have an extra copy or two to sell.

■ Check out all the sources described in the previous two sections.

It is not necessary to make notes in the margins of books or to underline crucial passages in magic marker.

If you want to do this, or if you feel it genuinely helps you, great. But it is by no means necessary. I have never underlined a single passage in a book or made a single note in a margin. But I know of plenty of intelligent people who do both and who tell me that they find them enormously helpful.

Some high school teachers teach their students these two habits, on the grounds that "they will be expected of you in college." Well, they won't be expected of you, and unless you personally benefit from either of these practices, there's no reason why you have to follow them.

The same advice applies to taking notes. Some high school teachers insist that their students take notes on everything, no matter how unimportant, because "you'll have to in college." This is simply not so. Of course, you should take notes in lectures where you are given factual information, and at any other time you feel you need to record what is being presented. But don't take notes just for the sake of taking notes, or because you think that's what a college student is supposed to do.

Save all your grade reports.

This is extremely important, for two reasons:

1. If your registrar errs on your transcript, you will, of course, want to correct it. This means that you must prove exactly how the registrar's office erred. With an official grade report as evidence, this will be easy.

2. Don't think the highly improbable will never happen to you, because it does happen to everyone occasionally. Your school could burn down, or a computer could mistakenly erase thousands of files. At one college where I have taught, there was a fire in the records office. Academic credits quite literally went up in smoke. Students whose records were destroyed and who could not provide proof of the credits they had earned suddenly found themselves first-semester freshmen again, with zero academic credits to their names.

Hang on to your grade reports forever—just in case.

College is where you learn to make choices.

This is something an old girlfriend of mine once told me when I was complaining about the pressures and contradictions of college life. It turned out that she had learned this piece of important wisdom from her mother, who had learned it from *her* grandmother.

The pressures, challenges, joys, and problems of college and college life will constantly present you with choices to make. Sometimes these choices will be difficult. Sometimes they will be choices you won't want to make at all—to flunk a test or to miss your girlfriend's birthday party, for example.

Being able to make wise decisions is one of the most important skills you can learn, and it is a skill that college will help teach you. Sometimes they will teach you the hard way—by making contradictory and irreconcilable demands on you or your time. Sometimes, happily, the choices will be easy ones. Either way, don't shy away from making decisions for yourself. The more experience you have making decisions, the easier it will be to make them, including big ones, for yourself in the future.

Don't let others make or try to make decisions for you.

The more freedom of choice you have, and the more choices you actually make for yourself, the more likely you are to determine your own future and to engineer your own happiness and success.

There is a certain comfort and security in having some other person or institution predetermine what you will do or how you will do it. After all, you don't need to think, choose, or take any responsibility in such a situation. But some of the most important things college can (and almost certainly will) teach you include how to think, how to choose, how to assume responsibility, and how to evaluate what you see, hear, and feel. If you don't want to learn these skills (and a great many people do not), you will probably be better off somewhere other than college.

Learn to use your intuition and your creative impulses.

Intuition and creativity are at least as important as logic, reason, and critical thinking. In many people's minds, including mine, they are *more* important—not just for spiritual and emotional growth, but also for intellectual growth, for one's general happiness and security, and for the simple ability to get along in the world from day to day.

College can be an ideal place to become aware of, to make use of, to strengthen, and to test your intuition and your creative abilities, both in and out of the classroom. Classes in the arts and humanities, in particular, can help train and build up your intuitive and creative faculties. I especially recommend classes that require you to create something yourself—classes in studio art, photography, crafts, music composition, drama, dance, film production, creative writing, and journalism.

These classes can be especially beneficial during your freshman and sophomore years, when you are still exploring and sorting out your different interests.

If you are afraid to take a class to develop your creativity because you may get a low grade, take the class anyway. Take it in pass/fail so that the risk is small. If this option is not available, be prepared to drop the class if you are doing badly in it. But give it a try—you might be surprised at how well you do and how much fun you have. Creativity, after all, comes naturally to everyone to some degree, and in introductory-level classes you are not going to be expected to perform like a pro but like an interested novice—which is exactly what you are.

If your experience at college is less than satisfying, or if you have doubts about your school or about college in general, you can always transfer out, take some time off, or drop out.

Once you have decided to go to college, you are not narrowing your options but broadening them. Once you have started school, you are never obliged to continue. You can always stop, either for a while or permanently. College should never be a four-year jail term. A great many options are *always* open to you, both in academia and outside it.

CHAPTER 3

Classes and Other Forms of Education

No one does all the work in a class. In fact, doing all the work in every class is virtually impossible.

If you are a full-time student, in most cases it will simply be impossible to do all the work for every one of your classes. This is all the more true if you have a part-time job or are a work-study student.

This is simply the way college is. Your classes will often make more demands on you than you can possibly fulfill. It is extremely important to realize this as quickly as possible. Your inability to keep up is not the result of stupidity or laziness but the result of unreasonable demands that your classes will make on you.

Do not expect or hope that these unreasonable demands will lessen or cease; they won't. Do not waste your time trying to change this system—it will frustrate and infuriate you and make your time that much more scarce.

These are your basic options for dealing with this situation. You can use more than one option at a time:

1. Attempt to do all the work demanded of you. This is, in most cases, fundamentally unrealistic.

2. Become a part-time student. If this is a genuine option for you, it is worth considering. However, if you take a half-time course load, you will need eight years to graduate. For many students, the thought of eight years in college is thoroughly unbearable. Also, many forms of financial aid are not available to part-time students.

3. Take a relatively small full-time course load. In most schools, twelve credits (or three courses) are the minimum required of a full-time student.

4. Take at least one, and preferably more, easy courses each term.

5. Cut corners.

Nearly everyone cuts corners in most or all of their classes on occasion. So do many teachers. But although this is practiced almost universally, and although students and teachers alike are very aware of it, it is rarely openly admitted or discussed.

There are many ways to cut corners.

a. Skim the reading assignment instead of going through it carefully. Often a ten-minute skim of an hour's worth of reading will teach you a surprising amount.

b. If you must research three different topics, do *not* research one of the topics thoroughly and ignore the others; this will leave you ignorant of two thirds of the material. Skimp on the amount of research in each area; this will give you at least a working knowledge in each area, and you may find, to your surprise, that you did enough research after all. ("Skimp" means "do somewhat less," not "do a small fraction.")

c. If you are not well prepared for a particular class meeting, keep your mouth shut. Do not risk entering into the discussion with your very limited knowledge. Your lack of preparation will likely be discovered very quickly. Stay out of the discussion unless you are called on; if you are called on, make as appropriate a statement as you can, but keep it short and conservative. Obviously, this suggestion does not apply to language courses.

d. If you are utterly unprepared for a class, simply do not show up for it. This option is to be used rarely, and only as a last resort. It should not be used for any class more than once (or at the very most twice) in a term.

e. It is all right and even recommended to cut corners in other areas of your life on occasion. It is fine to skip a meal or lose an hour or two of sleep once in a while so you can do a little extra studying. However, for your sanity and health, this must not be done regularly. More than once or at most twice a week is too much.

These are some ways in which you should never cut corners:

a. Never turn a paper in late without first getting permission to do so.

b. Never write a paper poorly or haphazardly.

c. Never cut a class when you are scheduled to make a presentation, or when you or your work will be at the center of attention.

d. Never cut class regularly.

e. Never show up late for class regularly.

f. Never fail to study for an exam or a test.

g. Never ignore a reading assignment completely. Skim it at least.

The problem with cutting corners is that you will not learn quite as much. You cannot, therefore, cut corners in the same class regularly and expect to keep up. The trick is to cut corners in one class during one week, and in another class the next.

"Cutting corners" means just that. It does *not* mean avoiding or ignoring most of the work in a class. You will still need to do at least 75 percent (or more) of the necessary studying and work in each class to keep up and do reasonably well. And you will, of course, need to attend each of your classes regularly.

Although corner-cutting is normally condoned when it is done privately and quietly, it is almost universally condemned when it is brought up openly. Never tell a teacher, administrator, or parent that you have cut corners unless you are asked quite directly if you have done so. Few will understand the necessity of corner-cutting, and most will feel you are lazy, selfish, or lacking in ability.

It may take some time before you get comfortable with cutting corners or before you can cut these corners efficiently and in the most beneficial manner. That's okay. With practice you will learn when, where, and how you can cut corners in the manner that works best for you. Cutting corners, in fact, is part of efficient studying. You will find, too, once you are out in the real world working full-time, that cutting corners properly and efficiently in your job may be necessary.

Cutting corners is *not* cheating, and it is not a sign of weakness or low ability. Nor should it be a cause for guilt. Keep your life as sane as you can and do your required work as best you can. Accept corner cutting as a necessity of college life. Remember, less than perfection is usually quite sufficient.

Teachers cut corners frequently also, but it is not always apparent. On occasion I have gone into classes totally unprepared, with no idea of what I would teach that day. Of course, since teachers are already familiar with their material, and since they often have years of experience, they are usually better able to vamp it than students.

Cutting corners is, of course, vastly preferable to cheating. Unlike cheating, cutting corners is legal and moral, and you still learn much about your subject. Unfortunately, some students try to do all the work in all their classes instead of cutting corners; they fall behind, and then they feel forced into cheating. But it is much smarter to cut some corners throughout the term than to resort to cheating. It's also more honest, less dangerous, and less stressful, and you will learn much more in the long run.

But be honest with yourself. Don't cut corners when you don't have to, and don't use it as an excuse for laziness.

A good teacher can make any subject interesting or intriguing; a poor one can make the most fascinating subject dull. The person teaching the class is far more important than the material the class will cover.

Avoid taking a class from a dull or unreasonable teacher, no matter how fascinating the subject may be to you. You will almost certainly wind up hating the class, and probably the teacher; you may also wind up losing your interest in the subject and possibly flunking the class to boot.

One of the main reasons people fail classes is because the teachers are dull, confusing, or unreasonable. Of course, if you do fail a class, the teacher will never be blamed for the failure—you will be.

Before you sign up for a course, or at least before you commit yourself irrevocably to it, interview the teacher and find out what the class will cover and what he or she is like. If there are several sections of the same class available, interview several teachers until you find one you like.

Once you have found a class that sounds interesting, find out who is teaching it. (If no teacher is listed in the class schedule, call up the department office and ask.) Call up that teacher and make an appointment with him or her in the teacher's office.

At the meeting, ask the teacher what the class will cover and what reading, lab work, and other projects and assignments will be involved. If you can get a copy of the syllabus to look at, so much the better. Ask any other questions you feel are appropriate, either about the course or the subject in general. If you strike up an interesting conversation with the teacher, terrific.

This may seem scary, especially for new students. But it is the teacher's job to help you learn. Most teachers are happy to help and to talk with you;

those who aren't willing are probably not worth taking a course from. Don't be afraid to interview any teacher in your college or university, no matter how learned or famous he or she may be.

The purpose of this interview is only partly to find out what the class will cover and entail. It also will give you a chance to see what the teacher is like, both as an instructor and as a human being. If he or she seems dull, disinterested, or eager to get you out of the office, then that teacher probably is one to avoid. Likewise, if the teacher seems more concerned with the work you will be required to do than with the material to be taught, I recommend you find a different teacher.

The ideal teacher seems friendly, open, helpful, and genuinely interested in the material he or she will be teaching.

If the conversation leads naturally to personal questions such as "What got you interested in this subject?," this usually is a good sign, regardless of which of you asks the question.

If you are attending a large university, or if the class you are thinking of taking is an introductory one, be sure to ask the teacher how much of the teaching will be done by TA's (teaching assistants or teaching associates). Sometimes the teacher is responsible only for a portion of the actual teaching, usually the lectures. If he or she will have a TA helping to teach the class, find out exactly what the TA will do. If the TA has more than minimal teaching responsibilities, learn who this person is. Then interview the TA in the same way you have just interviewed the teacher.

(If there is more than one TA, interview as many as you need to, until you find one you like. Then arrange to be in his or her class or section.)

Use your intuition as well as your rational judgment in picking an instructor. If you have a bad feeling about a teacher, even if you can't explain why, you should strongly consider looking for a different instructor.

Remember that the best teachers are the most responsive and interesting ones—not necessarily the easiest graders, the ones that will require the least work, or the ones that have been teaching the longest.

Interviewing teachers, and picking an interesting and competent one, are especially important for required classes—classes that you do not especially want to take and that you are taking only because your school insists that you do. With the wrong teachers, these classes can be the most boring and agonizing ones of your college career. With the right teacher, however, you may find yourself getting interested in (and even enjoying) a subject that used to leave you disinterested and bored.

It may seem quite time-consuming to interview the teacher of every class you are considering taking—and, indeed, it *will* take a fair amount of time. But in the long run it can save you tremendous amounts of time, anxiety, and boredom, and it can even make the difference between failing a class and getting an A. If you wind up with a dull or narrow-minded teacher, the class will in turn be dull, and very likely a waste of your time. But if you take the time to choose good teachers, your classes will be far more interesting, you will enjoy yourself far more, you will learn a great deal more, and your grades will likely be higher.

Be especially careful in choosing an instructor for freshman composition and other writing classes.

Freshman comp (sometimes called Freshman English) and other composition classes teach you the most accepted way to write college papers and exams, and thus these courses are some of the most useful and important ones of most students' college careers.

However, the teachers of freshman composition (and often of other writing classes) are usually the lowest-paid, and often the least experienced teachers in the entire college or university. They can often be the poorest instructors, and they are often the ones most likely to make mistakes.

Of course, some freshman comp teachers are excellent; some have had a great deal of experience; and some may be among the finest teachers in the school. However, because so many of them are inexperienced, and because they are so poorly paid, it is very easy to get a composition teacher who will do a poor job.

You should therefore use extra care in interviewing composition instructors. Use the same criteria outlined in the previous section.

It is not necessary to ask a teacher how long he or she has been teaching. Experience is not important. Some teachers do well from the first time they stand up in front of a classroom; others never do a good job, even after thirty years of teaching. Attitude and ability are far more important than experience.

To a lesser degree, all of this information applies to the instructors of introductory classes in other subjects, and to all TA's

Before enrolling in a class, try to talk with students who have had that teacher before.

This is worth doing if it can be done easily and conveniently. Your own interview with a teacher should enable you to make a pretty good judgment about that teacher, but it never hurts to ask a friend how that teacher performed in a previous class. Sometimes a teacher can act one way in the classroom and another way in a private conversation in his or her office. Weigh the comments of others carefully, but your own judgment (based on your interview) should be given higher priority.

If possible, talk to two or three people who have had the teacher before, rather than only one. This gives you a more balanced viewpoint, and allows for the variation of personal relations. It is quite possible that one student could despise a teacher that another student found fascinating. The judgments of any one student should be taken with a grain of salt. However, I have found that if two or more students feel a teacher is terrible or wonderful, they are usually correct.

Before you enroll in a class, find out what books will be required, and look through them briefly.

Books can be as fascinating or as tedious, as expert or as incompetent, as teachers.

Once you have picked out the

classes you want to take, go to your college bookstore to see what books will be required for those classes. Look through each book, check out the table of contents, and open the book at random and read a sample page. This will not only give you more of an idea of the content of the course, it will tell you how easy the book will be to get through.

Do not, however, expect most of your course books to be fascinating or even absorbing.

This advice does not apply to basic language texts or to texts in the sciences. These are often impossible to follow at first because they are technical; once you take the course, you will be learning everything you will need to know to make the book comprehensible.

Judge a course only by its required texts. Recommended books are just that—recommended and not required.

Important: Each teacher makes his or her own decision on what textbooks will be used in the class. Different sections of the same class taught by different instructors will often require different textbooks. Make sure that you are looking at the books for the section and instructor you are interested in.

Looking through textbooks can also help lead you to a good teacher. You may find it useful to browse through the textbooks for different courses, or for different sections of the same course. When you come upon a book that looks intriguing or even fascinating, this may be a course worth taking.

Before registering, try to look through a copy of the syllabus for each class you are thinking of taking.

A syllabus is a brief written outline of what a course will entail and what will take place at each class meeting.

The syllabus for a class is available from the teacher of that class. Not all teachers use them. If no syllabus is available, do not take this as a negative sign.

A request for a syllabus should *never* replace the personal interview you will have with each potential instructor. A good time to ask for a syllabus is near the end of such an interview.

If several different teachers are teaching different sections of the same class, each teacher will have his or her own unique syllabus.

If possible, sit in on some classes (preferably during the term before you would take them yourself) to see what they and their instructors are like.

This can be enormously beneficial and can save you a great many headaches and painful surprises. Once the class schedule for the following term has been published, look through it as soon as possible and make a list of the courses you are interested in taking. Find out who will be teaching those classes. Then approach each of these teachers and ask his or her permission to sit in on one of the teacher's classes during the current term.

Most teachers are happy to honor this request. However, a surprisingly large number of instructors will refuse to allow you to sit in on their classes; some will even be offended that you asked. If a teacher refuses, suggest that he or she choose the session you will attend, and say that you would be happy merely to watch rather than participate. Sometimes the instructor will allow you to visit under these terms.

There are many reasons why some teachers do not allow visitors in their classes, and their refusal to allow you to visit does not mean they are poor or dull teachers. If a teacher refuses to allow you to visit but gives a decent explanation why, or if he or she makes an alternative suggestion such as an office discussion, then I would not count this teacher out. If, however, he or she takes offense at your request or simply says "absolutely not" without an explanation, then chances are this person isn't worth taking a class from.

Remember that the style, focus, and content of a class can differ widely from one instructor to the next. Therefore, sitting in on Principles of Government taught by Instructor A will tell you nothing about what Principles of Government taught by Instructor B will be like.

Take the classes you want to take. Do not take a class just because your parents, teachers, or advisers tell you it will be good for you.

You are in college entirely for your own benefit—not anyone else's. You are there partly to find new interests, partly to explore interests you already have. As much as possible, feel free to pursue those interests—both old and new— without outside interference. Don't let others make your decisions or choose your courses for you.

Of course, most colleges have some required courses and/or distribution requirements for a certain number of classes to be taken within certain general areas of study. These are requirements for graduation, and if you want to graduate from that college, you will have to choose some of your courses with these requirements in mind. Also, your major may require that you take certain courses. But beyond these limitations, college will be most valuable—and most fun—if you alone choose the courses you take.

This does not mean you should ignore the advice of parents, teachers, advisers, or other students. Such advice can be valuable; consider it carefully, and actively seek it out when you feel need of it. But it is only *advice*—not orders.

Many teachers (and some advisers and parents) will strongly urge you to take classes they are interested in or that proved most helpful or valuable to them. Most teachers feel that everyone in general and you in particular would be better off getting interested and involved in precisely the things they are interested and involved in. In making this sort of recommendation, however, these people are forgetting that they are not you and that you have your own unique needs and interests. Do not let other people's ideas—even if they are presented with great conviction or even certainty—get in the way of your own real interests.

Don't sign up for a class in the hope it will discipline you, or straighten you out, or force you to study harder or change your life-style.

This doesn't work.

Parents love to encourage (or force) their sons and daughters to take certain classes—or even go to certain colleges—

for these reasons. Sometimes students will follow the same logic, hoping that by taking a hard or demanding class they will miraculously "shape up."

This is almost always nothing but wishful thinking and it doesn't work, because the attempted "solution" doesn't really address the problem.

If you are not studying hard enough now, then taking classes that require even more studying is not going to make you study harder. More likely they will make the efforts you *are* making seem more trivial. And keeping up will be that much harder, if not impossible. The likely result will be discouragement and failure—more than before.

If you need to change your habits or life-style, that change will take place only if you want it to and only if you decide that you can and will change.

Do not take a class you are not interested in just because somebody else recommended it, or because a friend of yours is in it.

Chances are very good that you will not enjoy such a class, that you will be bored by it, that you will learn little, and that you will do poorly in it. This remains true no matter who recommended it, and no matter who else is in it with you.

Don't schedule more than two classes in a row unless one of them is a fun class.

There is only so much a human being can learn without a break, and there are limits to everyone's energy and attention. Usually after two difficult classes in a row, you will be tired, anxious, or restless in class number three. Chances are you won't learn as well, enjoy the class as much, or do as well as if you had had a break.

Never schedule more than three classes in a row without a break under any circumstances unless they are all phys ed classes. Four or more classes in a row simply exceeds the normal limits of human attention and endurance.

Try to schedule your classes and your studying for those times when you are most attentive and do your best work. Avoid scheduling studying and classes for times when your level of energy and attention is low.

If you are a night person, take night classes; if you function poorly at night, take day classes.

This is not always possible, of course, and the time of day at which a class is held is not as important as who is teaching the class and how interested you are in the subject.

If you have to work, study, or take classes all day, avoid scheduling a class for the late afternoon or evening.

Sometimes this simply cannot be helped—but avoid the situation if you can. You will most likely be worn out. Your attention span will be shorter, you'll learn less, and you won't enjoy the class as much as you might have otherwise. You will likely be antsy, and you may find yourself counting the minutes until the class is over. And of course you probably won't do particularly well in such a class. This is very often true no matter how good your intentions were at first and no matter how much you originally wanted to take the class.

Do not take any class that starts before 10 A.M. unless you know you can get there on time and without losing sleep.

Be honest with yourself. If you are a late sleeper, you are not likely to get to an early-morning class on time, or at all, no matter how much you enjoy the class and no matter how strong your resolve.

Do *not* sign up for an early-morning class in the hope that this will force you to get up earlier. It rarely works and usually results in frequent absences or lateness. And even if it does manage to get you up and into the classroom, chances are you'll be so sleepy during the class that you'll learn little, do poorly, and not enjoy the class. And you might fall asleep in class.

You can get into many closed classes.

This is not especially difficult, and it will work in nine out of ten cases.

If you are told that a class has been closed, go to the registrar's office and ask for a Permission of Instructor form. Virtually every school has such forms, though they sometimes have different names. Some schools have a line on the regular course registration form for the instructor's signature, in which case the registration form also serves as a Permission of Instructor form.

Once you have this form, visit the instructor of the class. Since you have already interviewed the teacher, he or she should remember who you are.

Explain to the instructor how interesting (or fascinating, if you really feel that way) the course sounds and how much you want to take it. Don't overdo it; be sincere. Explain that the course has been filled (often the instructor will be unaware of this) and ask if you can become a member of the class. If the instructor agrees, ask him or her to sign the Permission of Instructor form. (If no such form is available, ask the instructor to write a note allowing you to take that course.) Take this signed form or the note to the registrar's office, and you will be allowed to sign up for the class.

You may prefer, if the circumstances warrant, to bring your Permission of Instructor form with you to your initial interview with the instructor. If you do this, however, do not mention until the end of the interview that the class has been officially closed. This gives the teacher the chance to get to know and like you, and it gives you the chance to learn whether you would like to take the class with that teacher.

If the teacher does not agree to sign the form or write a note, explain how much you want to take the class. Say that if someone drops out of the class you would like to take his or her place. Ask the teacher if he or she would put your name on a waiting list for the class; if the instructor has not established such a list, ask him or her to start one, with your name first.

If the instructor suggests that you put your name on the waiting list kept by the department or by the registrar's office, explain that they are very unreliable about keeping and following such lists. (This is almost universally true, and probably the teacher will be sympathetic.)

At this point you should go one step

farther, whether or not the instructor agrees to put you on his or her waiting list. Ask if you can sit in on the first few class sessions. Explain that if nobody has dropped out after the second week of classes, you will simply stop coming. Most instructors will agree to such a request, and many are impressed by it. By sitting in on the first few class sessions you demonstrate your interest in the class, you become a natural part of the class from day one, and you will be able to keep up with the class. When you do join the class officially, there will be no mad scramble to catch up—you will already be in gear with the other class members.

I do not believe I have *ever* been in or taught a class where someone did not drop out during the first two weeks. This means that your chances of getting into any closed class are pretty good to excellent. Even if enough people do *not* drop out by the end of the second week to give you an official spot in the class, by that time the instructor will be used to your presence. If at this point you ask politely if you can remain in the class, chances are good that he or she will be willing to bend the rules a bit and allow you to enroll officially, even though your presence in the class puts its size over the limit.

If the registrar's office offers to let you put your name on a waiting list, do so. Be sure to put down your phone number (if you work, put down both your home and work phones). If you are not offered the chance to do this, ask to do so. However, once you have done all this, do not expect anything to come of it. Go straight to the teacher of the course and follow the instructions I've given.

Never try to get permission from the registrar or anyone at a registration table to get into a closed class. They have no power to do anything for you, and they will only frustrate you. Often people at registration will tell you that there is nothing that they or you can do, that the class is closed, and you simply cannot get into it under any circumstances. *They are wrong*, no matter how much they might insist they are correct. They may even tell you that there is no such thing as a Permission of Instructor form. Ignore them, go to the teacher of the class, and follow the procedure I've outlined.

No matter how much you may have wanted to get into a class, and no matter how much effort it may have taken to be admitted finally, if you decide that you wish to drop the class, that is your right.

If a course requires a prerequisite, you can often get that prerequisite waived.

Do not be intimidated by prerequisites listed in catalogs and class schedules. They are almost never absolutes.

The purpose of a prerequisite is to make sure that all the students in the class have sufficient background or understanding or savvy to grasp the course material. If you can convince the instructor that you are capable of keeping up with the rest of the class, even though you do not have the official prerequisites, he or she usually will allow you to take the class. (Note: the waiving of prerequisites is the prerogative of the instructor.)

If there is a course you would like to take but do not have the prerequisites for, mention this at the *end* of your interview with the instructor.

Do not merely ask for the waiver; also be able to explain why you feel the waiver is appropriate. Some good reasons include:

■ You took a class somewhat similar to (or more advanced than) the prerequisite required, either at the same college you are in now or at a different institution.

■ You have done a fair amount of reading or study in the subject on your own.

■ You have done an independent study project or internship in the general area. This need not have been done in association with a college.

■ You audited the prerequisite class, either officially or unofficially. (See the section on auditing later in this chapter.)

Usually it is not necessary to have studied precisely the same material covered by the prerequisite; often it is enough to have some background in the same general area.

If there is more than one section of a particular class, and the instructor of one section refuses to waive a prerequisite for you, try a different instructor.

Sometimes prerequisites can be avoided by passing a short exam. These are usually (but not always) essay exams, usually lasting about thirty to sixty minutes. If the teacher of a course will not waive a prerequisite for you, but you feel you know enough that the prerequisite should be waived, ask if such an exam is offered. To play it safe, ask the same question of the secretary of the department, and of someone at your school's testing office.

If you feel you have the necessary background for a course but do not have the official prerequisite, a simpler but riskier option is open to you. Just sign up for the course. The people and computers that process registration forms almost never check to see if a student has a prerequisite; that task is left up to the individual instructors. So if you sign up for a course and there is space in it, you will almost always be officially registered for it.

What makes this option risky is that the instructor may check whether class members have the required prerequisite. If the instructor *does* check, you will either have to lie (this is not recommended) or present your case to him or her then. The worst that can happen is that you will be asked to leave the class.

One word of warning here: if you are *not* fairly sure that you have sufficient background or knowledge to take a class, you should not sign up for it, whether you have the appropriate prerequisite or not. You will very likely be in over your head very quickly, with relatively little chance of catching up. Instead, first augment your background in the subject, either through another course, or informal study on your own. Or you can sign up for the course as an auditor. (See the section on auditing later in this chapter.)

Many so-called required courses can be avoided entirely.

As with the waiving of prerequisites, the key issue here is whether you already have more or less the same background that the required course would give you.

The simplest and most direct way of getting out of required courses is to make your request directly to your department head (in the case of a requirement for a major) or your dean (in the case of distribution requirements, or requirements for graduation). Explain how and why your background in the subject is equivalent to what is taught in the required course. If the dean or department head feels your request is legitimate, he or she will waive the required course for you.

Most colleges will accept certain scores on the nationally standardized advanced placement tests as sufficient to waive a required course. Some schools will accept certain scores on the SAT's or ACT's as grounds for waiving required courses.

Some colleges will administer their own placement or exemption tests through a testing office and/or through the individual departments. Often a sufficiently high score on such a test will get you out of a required course. Deans may not be aware of these tests, so even if your dean tells you that no such tests exist, call up the testing office *and* the department in which the course you wish to avoid is being offered. Ask them about the possibility of placing out of the required course by taking a placement or exemption exam.

Some of these exams may be repeated. If you fail such an exam, ask if and when you can take it again. Often with a little studying, you will pass the exam on the second or third try. Of course, it never hurts to do a little extra studying before you take the exam the first time, either.

Bending the rules on required courses can take several different forms, depending on the school and the circumstances:

1. The course requirement is waived.

2. The course requirement is waived and credit for the class you are avoiding is awarded to you.

3. The course requirement is waived and credit for the class you are avoiding is awarded to you; you must, however, pay the regular tuition for the credits you are being awarded, even though you are not taking the class.

4. Your choice of 1 or 3, as you prefer.

5. The requirement for that course is waived, but you must substitute a higher-level course in the same department or area of study.

It is extremely important to remember that although a rule is printed as an absolute in the catalog (for example, that all students must take one year of a foreign language), it may still be waived under certain circumstances (if, for example, you already speak a foreign language fluently).

You can bend any rule in a class or have any exception made if the instructor will give permission.

In a sense, a class is the teacher's kingdom; he or she decides what goes on in that class, and, except for activities that might be illegal, immoral, or against the college's own rules, the teacher's decision usually is final.

Therefore, if you feel that you need

or deserve an exception to your teacher's general rule or policy, ask him or her. Be straightforward and sincere; make your request and give your reasoning. The instructor will grant or refuse your request as he or she sees fit. Most instructors try to be as fair as possible in making such decisions, though of course they may not always see your situation as you do or be as sympathetic as you had hoped. (This topic is discussed in some detail in Chapter 7.)

If your college does not offer a class in a topic you are interested in, you can probably arrange an independent study in it.

Most colleges permit their students to take at least one independent study course per term. Some offer a predetermined array of independent study projects, but you can still design an independent study course of your own choosing.

If you can get a faculty member to agree to sponsor and supervise an independent study project, you can complete that project for academic credit. Simply go to a teacher you feel might be interested, explain your proposed project, and ask if he or she would be willing to help you.

You may have to go to several teachers to find one who will agree to sponsor the project, because many teachers prefer not to sponsor independent studies, and others simply may not have the time. Do not give up, however; if one teacher turns you down, ask him or her to recommend someone else who might be willing and able to work with you.

If you do not know which teachers

to ask, ask the secretary or the head of the appropriate department or departments. Often they can make recommendations. At worst, you can always get a list of the instructors in the department, along with their phone numbers and office hours, and you can simply go down the list until you find someone you like who is willing to sponsor you.

When you explain your project to a potential teacher, you do not have to provide a complete list of proposed readings or explain what your final project for the course will be. On the other hand, do not be so vague as to leave the nature of the project in doubt. For example, you need not say, "I want to do a comparison of Poe and Stephen King, and I want to read these fifteen books," though there is nothing wrong with being this specific. "I want to compare one nineteenth-century and one twentieth-century horror writer" usually will do. "I want to do a project on horror," however, may be too unfocused to get an instructor's approval.

Sometimes you may have to negotiate with an instructor about the focus, content, or required work in an independent study course; he or she will have certain suggestions and ideas that are not thoroughly congruent with your own. In general, if the instructor suggests changes you do not find too bothersome or difficult, or that do not alter the basic nature of the study project, you should probably go along with his or her changes. If, however, the instructor suggests changes that make the project into something you do not want to pursue, simply thank the teacher for his or her interest and seek another faculty sponsor.

As you explain your project, the teacher is essentially interviewing you to see if he or she will enjoy working with you—so dress neatly, be friendly, and in general try to act in a pleasant manner. At the same time, try to get a feel for the instructor to see if you will like working with him or her.

Independent studies are one of the best and most fun ways to learn what you want to learn. You can work at your own pace to some degree, and you can study at whatever times and in whatever manner work best for you. Independent studies provide you with the opportunity to work closely one-on-one with an instructor. If the instructor is good, this is tremendously valuable. Independent studies in general also teach you to work and think well on your own.

You should know that independent studies require real work and sincere effort on your part, and that there is virtually no way you can fake your way through them. It will be just you and the instructor; there will be no other students to hide behind.

Some schools limit the number of independent study credits you may earn per term or the number that may be applied toward your major or degree. Check with your registrar for details.

Internships are one of the best ways to gain experience, make professional contacts, prepare for a career, and learn a great deal about a specific field while earning college credits.

An internship is a brief stint working for a company, a public-service organization, an individual involved in a particular profession, or some other person or organization outside college.

Although internships often can involve hard work, they can teach you a great deal more about a particular profession or field, and immensely more about the world outside college than any course that meets inside a classroom.

Internships involve a specified amount of time (usually six to ten hours per week) working for an individual or organization. Usually interns have regular hours during which they must be at their assignments, just as if they were employees. Some interns *are* employees—they are paid for their time and effort.

Interns learn through experience what a particular field (professional, artistic, or otherwise) is really like. By working with professionals as an intern, you will also learn what makes the field tick and how to break into it. You will also quickly drop any illusions you had about the field. Even more important, the experience will help you decide whether it is something you genuinely want to explore further or go into as a career. This can save you rude shocks later.

But internships have two even more important benefits:

First, you will meet a good number of professionals in a particular field. These contacts can be tremendously helpful in the future, especially if you have performed well as an intern. These people can give you inside information about the field; they can tell you about job openings and job possibilities in the field; and they can serve as references for future jobs.

Second, interns often become employees, sometimes immediately after the internship ends. Quite often, if the intern has done a good job, he or she will be asked to stay with the organization as a regular salaried employee, either as soon as he or she graduates, or immediately.

You should know two things about internships, however. First, internships are almost always hard work. Slacking off is not permitted, and in many cases the pace of work can be swift, even frantic. After the first week or two you will be expected to keep up with the pace of the organization.

Second, most internships are not glamorous. If you intern at a magazine, for example, you will most likely be a combination gofer, office boy/girl, and typist. If you intern with a local politician, your job will likely be to answer the phone, type letters, and keep track of your boss's schedule. Interns usually are near or at the bottom of the pecking order, and they often get the dirtiest and most menial jobs. Your duties may include emptying the wastebaskets, cleaning the bathrooms, or making coffee.

Still, even being low man or woman on the totem pole affords you the opportunity to work with professionals in their field, and you will still learn an immense amount about that field.

Internships usually last one full semester, though sometimes they can be arranged for longer periods. Academic credit is awarded for both paid and unpaid internships. Speaking generally, you can expect to receive one academic credit for every two to three hours of time you spend per week as an intern.

Many colleges and universities have a formal or informal apprenticeship program. But even if your school has no such program, you can generally arrange an internship yourself and receive academic credit for it.

Schools with formal internship programs usually have an internship office. This office keeps in contact with a wide variety of local and national organizations that accept interns. Often the internship office provides interns to organizations on an ongoing basis. For example, the office might arrange for a different student each term to intern somewhere within General Mills. The internship office keeps a list of internship opportunities available, and you can look through the list for the internship that suits you best. Usually schools with an internship office have a regular course code number for registering for an internship, and usually internships are available (or at least permitted) in most or all of the departments.

Other schools have internship programs within particular departments. If you want to do an internship in, say, social work, and your school has no internship office, check with the Social Work Department (or the Urban Affairs or Sociology Department).

Still other schools have no formal internship program, but they allow students to arrange internships on their own. These schools usually have a standard course code number for internships for registration purposes. Normally a teacher must agree to sponsor or supervise the internship; this can involve nothing more than signing a form, or it may involve monitoring and evaluating the student's performance as an intern.

If your college (or a particular department) has an internship program offering a specific list of internships, you are not limited to that group of internships. You can still arrange an internship of your choice with any organization you wish, provided you can get the approval of that organization and of one instructor.

Sometimes internships arranged through a college department or internship office are very easy to get. At other times certain internships may be very much in demand. You may be asked to make a formal written application for some internships, and/or you may be asked to be interviewed. (Treat all such interviews as if they were job interviews: dress formally and bring a resume.) Only a small percentage of the applicants for these internships may be accepted for them, so do not be overly disappointed if you did not get the internship you wanted. You may be able to arrange a similar internship with a different organization on your own.

If your school has no internship program and if it does not even have a course code to use for registering for an internship, you can still do an internship. Simply register for an independent study course (following your school's specific regulations), and let your internship be the content of that independent study course.

Arrange an internship on your own as follows:

1. First, decide whom you want to intern for or what general field you want to intern in. Prepare a list of at least three or four possible sponsoring organizations. The Yellow Pages are fine for picking these. If you do not have access to a car, be sure the places you choose are accessible by public transportation or on foot. If there is a decent chance that the internship will involve evening hours, be sure to check that any necessary public transportation runs during those hours.

2. Decide what hours you have available for the internship. This might be one eight-hour day per week, six hours one day per week, three or four hours two afternoons a week, etc. It helps immensely to know the rest of your class schedule before setting up an internship, but this is not always possible. The ideal times for interning are when you have little or nothing else you must do. One word of caution: you will also have to arrange your interning hours so they are convenient for the sponsoring organization. Decide which hours will be best for you, but be flexible.

3. Find a faculty sponsor. This can be any teacher in a department closely related to the field in which you will be interning. If you are interning in a public-relations firm, your sponsor might come from the Business Department or the English Department. If you are interning for HUD, your sponsor might come from the Government, the Sociology, the Urban Planning, or the Public Affairs Department.

You may need to talk to several different instructors before you find one willing to sponsor your internship. Be patient and don't get discouraged; many teachers simply do not have the time to serve as sponsors, and others may simply not be interested. You may want to ask the secretary or head of the appropriate department for the names of some instructors who might be most willing to be sponsors. At worst, you can just get a list of instructors in the appropriate department, along with their phone numbers and office hours, and you can go down the list until you find someone who will serve as your sponsor.

Once you have a list of potential faculty sponsors, call the first one and make an appointment for an interview. During the interview, explain that you would like to be an intern in a particular field, give the instructor the list of organizations you would like to approach, and ask if he or she would be willing to sponsor the internship.

There may be some details to work out at this point. The teacher may ask that you turn in some kind of written work at the end of the term, or he or she may ask that someone in the sponsoring organization write up a brief evaluation of your work at the end of the internship. (If the instructor wants such a write-up, be sure you do get one when your internship is complete, or you may not receive credit for it.)

What you are seeking here is the instructor's verbal approval of your general plan, and/or his or her verbal agreement to sponsor the project once you have arranged it with the outside organization.

Once you have secured this, you can proceed.

Note: my warnings regarding dull or narrow-minded teachers do not apply here. Because the role of a teacher in an internship is small, you need not like the instructor who sponsors your internship, and he or she need not be a good teacher.

4. Call up the organizations you are interested in interning for, starting with the one you are most interested in. Although you should explain things in your own words, say something like this:

"Hi. My name is _____. I'm a student at _____. I'm very interested in the _____ field, and I'm planning to do an internship this/next term. I've already got faculty approval of the internship, and I'd very much like to be able to intern with you. I can volunteer _____ hours of my time per week for all of this/next term, and I'm willing to work at whatever tasks you assign me. I want to learn about the _____ field through working experience in it while I earn college credits."

If you have a skill that directly pertains to the internship, you should mention it—for example, "I can type fifty words per minute" or "I know BASIC and FORTRAN."

If you are contacting a large organization, direct your inquiry to a particular department. For instance, if you are interested in the marketing of consumer goods and you call up General Mills, ask for the Marketing Department.

Often you may be referred from one person to another before you find someone who is interested; this is fairly normal, so be patient. If someone is interested, they will probably ask you quite a few questions; answer these freely and openly. Then you may be called in for an interview, just as if you had applied for a job.

If you leave a message and your call is not returned within twenty-four hours, call back. If you must do this three or four times and your call is still not returned, move on to the next organization.

It is all right to contact several organizations at once about internships. However, except in very unusual circumstances, you can do only one internship at a time.

Do not expect the first organization you contact to accept you as an intern. You may have to make five or even fifteen telephone calls, or have several interviews before someone offers you an internship. Be patient and keep plugging.

A good spot for doing an internship might even be one of the offices within your own college or university.

5. Once you have made arrangements with the sponsoring organization, go back to your sponsoring teacher and tell him or her of the arrangements you have made. Then secure that teacher's official approval.

6. Register for the internship or independent study.

Internships that you arrange yourself normally do not pay a salary, nor should you ask for one unless the organization seems to indicate that they might be willing to pay one.

Other important information about internships:

Large corporations perform many different functions and have many different departments, so they may be appropriate for many different kinds of internships. For example, Pillsbury has a Research Department, a Consumer Affairs Department, a Transport Department, an Advertising Department, a Packaging Department, a Computer Department, a Finance Department, a

Bookkeeping Department, a Planning Department, a Personnel Department, and so on.

Most schools allow you to do more than one internship during your college career. Some set certain limits, however. Be sure to check with your registrar to learn the particular regulations of your school.

Many internships do not require academic work. Some schools or instructors, however, may require you to write a paper analyzing the field, keep a journal of your experiences as an intern, or produce some other form of written work. Be sure to be clear about the academic requirements of your internship, if any, when you arrange it with your faculty sponsor.

Some organizations offer five-day-a-week, full-time internships for students. These internships usually pay a salary, and the competition for them is quite stiff. Obviously, if you intern in such a program, you must temporarily put aside your regular studies. Different schools will award very different amounts of academic credit for this type of internship, ranging from none to fifteen credits per term.

An internship is especially useful and beneficial during your senior year; it can help you make the transition from school to work, and it may lead to a job offer. Ideally, I recommend one internship early in your college career, and another during your senior year.

Some schools will allow you to receive credit for doing volunteer work.

A few schools have regular programs wherein you can do volunteer work for a hospital, clinic, counseling center, Red Cross office, or other public-service organization and receive credit for your efforts. These organizations may either be within your college or in the general community. Essentially such volunteer work boils down to internships under another title. Volunteer work, however, is often easier to get.

If your school has no such program, you may be able to arrange to be a volunteer nurse's aid, crisis counselor, or such yourself. Follow the suggestions in the preceding section on internships.

Independent studies and internships can improve your chances of getting into a graduate or professional school, or of getting a job in your field.

The old saying "experience is the best teacher" is very true, and many employers, professional schools, and graduate schools know it. If you have spent some time as an intern working in the world outside college for a professional organization, this will be a feather in your cap. As an intern, you will have had some practical experience and training, as well as some familiarity with the field's day-to-day functioning—not just theoretical knowledge. Likewise, independent-study projects show that you are capable of working, thinking, and completing projects on your own. This is a very important qualification for many jobs and for many kinds of graduate and professional study.

Auditing a course enables you to learn whatever you want to learn with no requirements and in the most relaxed atmosphere possible.

If there is a course you are interested in but are hesitant to take because it may be too demanding, because you have no background in it, or because you feel you may not be able to keep up with or do well in it, you should think about auditing that course.

Auditing a course means that you attend the class meetings simply because you are interested in the subject. You receive no grade or academic credit for auditing a class, and usually you have no obligation to complete any of the work, but you still have the opportunity to learn about the subject. You are an observer and (to varying degrees, depending on the particular class and instructor) a participant, but you will not be evaluated in any official manner. Depending on your school and your arrangement with the instructor, your transcript will either make no mention of your having taken the class, or (in most cases) it will show that you have taken the class, and your grade in that class will be listed as "audit."

Auditing a course is an excellent way to familiarize yourself with a subject without risking academic failure. This can be of enormous benefit: you can see how strong your interest in a subject genuinely is, and you can beef up your background enough so that next term you can take a class in that subject for credit and likely do well in it. Auditing a course is also an excellent way to get to know a teacher, or to evaluate and choose teachers for future terms.

The role of an auditor will differ from teacher to teacher and from class to class. In some classes, you might be permitted to participate and attend as much or as little as you wish. In others, there might be a limit on how much you are permitted to participate—for example, the instructor might permit you to attend lectures but not discussions or labs. Still other teachers will ask for a certain minimum degree of participation from auditors. For example, a teacher may ask that you attend classes regularly and keep up with the reading. In a few classes (studio art classes, for example, where there is little point in being a mere observer) you might even be asked to complete all the work a regular student would. Each instructor has the right to establish such guidelines for auditors as he or she sees fit. You should either agree to these guidelines and follow them, try to work out some agreeable compromise, or not audit the class at all. Do *not* agree to certain things and then ignore them later.

In a similar way, the amount of instruction and help an auditor receives can vary greatly from one instructor or class to the next. Some teachers treat an auditor no differently from a regular student: they provide auditors with one-to-one consultations and assistance whenever the auditors request it, and they thoroughly critique and evaluate any work the auditor chooses (or is asked) to turn in. Some teachers will even provide you with a written evaluation of your performance in the class. This evaluation is, of course, unofficial.

Other teachers will allow an auditor to sit in on lectures and discussions but will not critique his or her work and will not provide much or any one-on-one assistance. This is entirely the teacher's prerogative. If you are an auditor and need help from your instructor, feel free to ask for it. But if the teacher refuses to give it, accept this refusal gracefully.

Although most teachers are happy to have auditors in their classes, occasionally a teacher will refuse to accept any auditors in a particular class. This is also very much the teacher's right.

Normally auditors are accepted into classes only if space remains in those classes after everyone who wants to take those classes for credit has already signed up.

If a course requires a prerequisite, often that prerequisite will not apply to auditors. (See the section, earlier in this chapter, on waiving prerequisites.)

Some schools or departments require auditors to obtain the official permission of their instructors; others allow you simply to sign up, just as you would for a credit class. The cost for officially auditing a class varies from college to college. Some colleges charge an auditing fee of between 10 and 60 dollars per class in place of tuition. Many charge a percentage (usually 50 percent) of the regular tuition for that class. A few charge the full tuition rate, and a few will charge nothing at all (though free auditing is usually provided only to students who are also enrolled in credit courses during the same term).

If you want to get the most out of auditing a class, follow the same general guidelines suggested for regular students: interview any teacher before signing up for his or her class, only audit a class that you genuinely have an interest in, don't audit a class if the teacher is a bore or a narrow-minded person, and so on.

Until now I have been discussing official auditing—auditing wherein you register for the course and pay the required fee to the college. If you simply want to learn about a particular subject and do not care whether that class appears on your transcript, you should seriously consider unofficial auditing.

In unofficial auditing you arrange to be an auditor directly with the instructor and leave the registrar and the rest of the college administration out of the picture entirely. Although many teachers will not go along with this, a good many will.

Arrange to audit a class unofficially as follows:

Make an appointment with the instructor of the class you want to audit. Dress neatly for the appointment, arrive on time, and be friendly and polite throughout the meeting. Explain to the instructor that you are interested in his or her class and that you very much want to study that particular topic. Explain also that you do not want or need academic credit for that class but that you want a chance to learn that particular material. Ask the teacher if he or she will allow you to sit in on the class informally as an auditor.

There is a decent chance that the teacher will agree to this, especially if he or she likes you.

Sometimes the instructor will not understand that you want to audit the course unofficially; he or she will ask to see proof of your registration, or will ask you to register officially as an auditor. If this occurs, meet with the teacher privately after class and explain that you had hoped to be able to audit the class unofficially. If the instructor asks why, you can be quite honest: "If I

registered as an auditor, it would cost
me _____ dollars; if we do it unofficially, it will save me that money." A
good number of instructors will be very
sympathetic to this and will agree to the
unofficial arrangement. If they don't,
though, and you still want to audit their
classes, then register and pay the appropriate fee.

Many—perhaps most—classes are boring.

That's the way college is. The trick
is *not* to settle for boring teachers and
classes, however, but to seek out those
teachers who are interesting, vibrant,
caring people. There are some at every
college; you just have to find them.

Don't expect every class to be dull.

Some students assume (and even
expect) that every class will be boring,
and they don't even hope that any of
their classes will be interesting or fun.
This is a big mistake—as big as assuming
that every class will be fascinating. Do
not fall into this despair—you will be
depriving yourself of the power of
choice, and you will make your life more
difficult than it needs to be. By carefully
selecting your teachers and educational
activities, you can make your college
years as useful and as enjoyable as
possible.

Be willing and ready to make changes, including major changes, in your schedule during the first two weeks of any term.

College has a way of dumping some
big and unpleasant surprises on students during the first weeks of the term,

and you can never be sure what they will be or where they will come from. The teacher who was so kind and friendly in his or her office may turn out to be pompous and narrow-minded in class. The text that hadn't come in by the time registration began may arrive during the second week of the term and turn out to be utterly incomprehensible. The work-study job you were promised may suddenly and mysteriously vanish, with only "We're sorry, we made a mistake" given as an explanation. Your TA may take an instant dislike to you for no reason you can figure out and may insult you in class and flunk both of your first two papers. And so on.

Such uncertainty and minor misery early in the term seem to be part of college life. Although such small disasters probably won't happen every term, there probably will be two or three terms during your college career when you will have to make many last-minute changes in your schedule and plans.

The number of credits awarded for a particular class is not necessarily proportionate to the amount of work required for that course.

This can vary tremendously from one class, teacher, or college to another. One teacher may require ten or even fifteen hours of work per week for his or her three-credit course; another may require only an hour or two for the same three credits. Sometimes there can even be a vast difference in the amount of work required for two different sections of the same course.

Speaking generally, the teacher has the right to require as much or as little work for a class as he or she wishes—

provided, of course, that the requirements are more or less the same for all the students in that class. However, the upper limit should be three hours of work (including time spent in classes and labs) per week per hour of credit awarded. If one of your teachers is requiring more, you may want to speak to him or her, or to his or her superior, about it. See Chapter 5 for more details.

In cases where the work required is not excessive for most students but is excessive for you (because you work more slowly, because you need time to absorb the material thoroughly, or for whatever reason), you are probably out of luck. Still, it wouldn't hurt to discuss the problem frankly with your teacher. Sometimes a solution can be worked out.

Refer also to the first section of this chapter, which explains how to cut corners.

Learn as soon as possible how to write college papers.

I cannot stress this strongly enough, especially for students majoring outside the natural sciences.

A great many of your college classes will require essay exams or papers, and your success in those classes will therefore depend a great deal on your ability to write those essays and papers properly.

A badly written paper brimming with careful thought and good ideas is often likely to be given a grade of C or lower. A well-written paper without much thought or understanding behind it will often get a high grade. Is this fair? In many ways, no. But is this really how it happens much of the time? Yes.

Being able to write papers and essays well will also help you to think and reason well, and it will help you to make careful and wise judgments.

For most students, learning to write well means taking one or more composition classes in their first term or terms as a college student.

Chapter 6 will explain in detail how to write a good college paper. It is not as hard as you think.

Avoid skipping any language or math classes.

In these classes, each class session builds directly on the material presented in the previous session. If you miss one class, you are already behind, and it will take some effort to catch up. If you miss two classes in a row, the catching up will take considerably more effort. If you miss three or more classes in a row, the catching up can often be nearly impossible.

Study immediately before class instead of (or in addition to) the night before. If this is not possible, study as soon before the class as you can.

You can forget a good deal during a night's sleep, and if you study just before class, the material will be fresh and clear in your mind. So will any questions you might need to ask. Also, studying followed immediately by a class meeting in the same subject can sometimes cause the material to sink in more deeply; the studying and the class reinforce one another.

But if you study immediately before the class, allow yourself enough time to get through the entire assignment.

Do not pretend to understand something you do not.

This may make you look intelligent in the short run, but it backfires. The teacher will proceed to the next point, leaving you confused, and if the next point is based on the thing you did not understand, you will be even more lost than before. If you do not understand something and it comes up on a test, you will get it wrong. And it makes things more awkward when you finally have to go to the teacher for help and admit you're lost.

If there is something in your class reading, lectures, or discussions you do not understand, *always* feel free to ask questions of your teacher or your TA. Their job is to help you learn, and part of this job involves responding to any questions you might have.

If you are afraid to ask a particular question in class, ask the instructor or TA privately afterward. You should *never* be embarrassed to ask *any* question pertinent to the class, especially if you ask privately. Likewise, if you are having difficulty in a class, feel free to ask your teacher or TA to give you additional help during his or her office hours. You should not be ashamed or hesitant to ask for this help; providing it is part of their job, and their office hours are in part set up for this very purpose. Any teacher or TA who refuses to provide additional help of this sort is not doing his or her job properly.

If you fall behind in a class by more than two weeks, or if you are

quite lost, you should probably drop the class—even if the teacher recommends otherwise.

There is a point at which you are far enough behind (or sufficiently lost or confused) that it is too late to catch up. When you reach this point, it is best to cut your losses and drop the class.

For most people, this point is about two weeks behind. Of course, it differs from person to person, but once this point is reached, it is a waste of time and energy to continue with the class.

If you discuss this problem with virtually any college teacher in the country, however, he or she will urge you to make your best effort to catch up and stick out the class. *This is almost universally bad advice.* In the majority of such cases, the student tries his or her best, still never catches up, and flunks. At this point, many teachers add insult to injury by saying, "It's your own fault."

Dropping a class does not make you a failure or a quitter. In fact, in the case where you're already quite a bit behind, dropping the class is usually the smartest thing to do.

If it looks likely that you will fail a course (or do worse than a C−), you should probably drop the course or change your status to that of an auditor.

A dropped course does not appear on your academic record at all; a course with a poor or failing grade appears as a blemish. You are best off cutting your losses and dropping any course you feel you are unlikely to pass. Keep track of the last day to drop classes; look at your progress in each of your classes and see if dropping any is appropriate.

There is another option open to you. Instead of dropping the class, see if your registrar will change your registration to that of an auditor. If you offically audit the class, you will receive no academic credit or grade for the course, so that you can remain in the class (if you wish) without having to complete all the work or perform at a certain level.

When you go to change your status to an auditor, speak with your instructor to let him or her know that you are changing your status, and to make sure you can fulfill his or her requirements (if any) for an auditor.

You can always take the course again once you have dropped it or become an auditor. And when you do take the class again, you will be several steps ahead of everyone else, since you will already have taken a part of that class before. This will make it much easier to receive a high grade the next time around.

Once you have decided to drop a class, do so officially and immediately.

If it is still early in the semester, the sooner you drop the course, the better chance you will have of replacing it with another class, and the less work you will have to do in that new class to catch up with the other students. If you are dropping a class and not replacing it with anything else, then the sooner you drop it, the larger the tuition refund for that class will be. Most schools refund a progressively smaller percentage of the tuition for dropped classes as the term wears on. After three to five weeks, usually no tuition is refunded.

Also, dropping a class promptly opens up a space for another student.

Adding a class without dropping one at the same time may also add to your tuition bill.

If you are already well into the term and are thinking seriously of dropping a course, check your school's regulations as to the last day a course can be dropped. Many schools will not let you drop a course after a certain day, or they may require special signatures from the instructor, your dean, or the appropriate department after a certain point. These signatures are usually—but not always—given routinely.

To drop a course officially, you must file a form with your school's registration office. Merely notifying the teacher, or simply not showing up, will not do the trick. If you do not let the registration office know you are dropping, you may find yourself at the end of the term with a failing grade in that class.

The same advice applies to internships and independent studies you are thinking of dropping.

You have no obligation to any teacher or to your college to do well in or even complete any class you take.

The purpose of college is to serve you, the student. You have no obligation to the college other than to pay it for its services and to respect its staff, grounds, buildings, and property. If a teacher or adviser says he or she is disappointed in you—because you did not follow his or her advice, or because he or she does not approve of your academic program or career choice, or because you flunked one or even all of your classes—do not take that disappointment too seriously.

You are not at college to live up to anyone else's expectations.

It is only natural that advisers and teachers will take personally some of your actions and decisions, academic or otherwise. Sometimes they feel it is their failure as well as yours if you flunk a class or do not do well in it. However, do not in turn take *their* reactions personally.

CHAPTER 4

Grades

Grades are not nearly as important as most students, parents, administrators, and teachers think.

Most students worry a great deal about grades. Some drive themselves crazy trying to get good ones, and some have nervous breakdowns because the grades they have gotten don't seem good enough.

Both students and their parents see high grades as the grand goal of college and as the necessary carrot on the stick of education. The truth is, however, that grades don't make a whole lot of difference, and very few people in your life are going to care about them.

Here are the only areas in which grades *do* mean something:

1. Grades are a fairly good indicator of how well you have mastered a subject and of how strong your abilities, potential, or achievement are in that subject. As such, they can be useful to you.

2. Your college grades are taken into account if you apply for scholarships or fellowships, or to graduate or professional programs.

3. Obviously, you need to achieve certain grades (usually a C− average as an undergraduate and a B− average as a student in a graduate or professional program) to receive credit for your classes and to graduate.

4. If you intend to transfer to another college, the schools you apply to will take your college grades into account.

5. You may need to keep up a certain grade point average to participate in school athletic activities, to join certain campus organizations or honor societies, or to receive certain kinds of financial aid.

6. High grades are, of course, a feather in your cap, and they can lead to your election to Phi Beta Kappa and other honor societies.

Beyond these considerations, however, few people in or outside of academia think or care about your grades, or are ever interested in knowing what they are.

Those people in academia who do care about your college grades care primarily about the grades you have earned in courses in your major field; second, about your grade point average during your junior and senior years; third, about your overall college grade point average; and last, about the grades you earned during your freshman and sophomore years.

The grades you earn as a freshman and sophomore are given comparatively little weight. This is precisely because it is understood that you spent much of your time during those years adjusting to college life, fulfilling basic requirements, exploring and sorting out your academic and professional interests, and building up a basic background in one or more areas of study.

The grades you receive in courses in your major are, however, taken *quite* seriously within academia, because your major field is supposed to be your field of greatest knowledge, wisdom, interest, ability, and expertise.

Oddly enough, I have found that the people who worry most about grades are the brightest students—the ones who need to worry about them least. I can still remember vividly a scene in my college dining hall. A woman was sobbing over a grade she had received in one of her classes. "I'm sorry," I said. "Did you flunk?" She said, "No, I got a B-plus." It turned out that she had never gotten anything less than an A before in her life.

Employers normally care very little about your college grades, and they will not normally ask to see them.

I have never had an employer or potential employer outside of academia ask me, even in the most general way, what any of my college grades were. It has always been enough for them that I have earned the appropriate degrees. If you plan to go into college teaching, you may find that some schools will ask to see transcripts as part of your job application; but otherwise employers seem to be disinterested in grades and GPA's. The truth is that, in general, your college grades tell employers little or nothing about what kind of a job you can or will do for them.

Never mention grades on your resume; it's not only unnecessary, it's also considered irrelevant and amateurish. However, if you have made Phi Beta Kappa or otherwise earned some other academic award or distinction, by all means list that on your resume.

The only organizations that care about your grades or that will ask to see them are schools, and organizations that administer scholarships and fellowships.

Generally you will need a GPA of 3.0 in your junior and senior years to be considered seriously for admission to a graduate or professional program. Again, speaking very generally, you will be expected to have earned a GPA of 3.2 in your junior and senior years to be seriously considered for medical school. Your GPA for courses in your major should be at least as high or higher.

There are exceptions, though. If you are a whiz in your field but otherwise not much of an academic, you are likely to be granted admission to a graduate program in your field even if your grades outside your major are not so great. And if you are applying to a graduate program in a field other than the field you majored in as an undergraduate, your grades in that subject will, of course, be looked at more carefully than the grades you earned in your major.

If you have been given a grade you feel is unfair, you can get it changed.

Grades are not handed down from God like the Ten Commandments. They represent your teacher's best evaluation of your achievement and ability—and teachers, like anyone else, can and do make mistakes and show poor judgment sometimes.

Sometimes the mistakes are simple errors in copying or record-keeping. I once had a student complain to me that she deserved a better course grade than I had given her. I looked in my records and saw that I had given her a B-plus—a grade I thought was quite appropriate. So I went through all her assignments with her and showed her why a B-plus was the proper grade. "But you didn't *give* me a B-plus!" she said finally. So I checked the computer printout on which I had submitted grades to the registrar. Sure enough, I had filled in the wrong grade by mistake. Of course, I apologized and gave her the B-plus.

So if you receive a grade on your report card that you genuinely feel is unfair or inappropriate, don't be frightened or embarrassed about seeing your instructor about it.

Make an appointment with the instructor to discuss your grade. Be sure to explain that this is the purpose of the meeting. Making an appointment is always better than just walking in—it gives teachers the chance to check their records, and it keeps them from feeling as if they are suddenly being accosted and accused. If the grade was given jointly by two instructors, or by an instructor and a TA, arrange to meet with both of them together.

When you arrive for the interview, be polite, pleasant, and neatly dressed. Act as if you are there to have a discussion, not an argument. Arrive on time, and bring all your papers, tests, and exams from that course. (Always save your graded papers, tests, and exams for precisely this purpose.)

First, check with your instructor that the grades on your papers, tests, and exams match those in *all* his or her records. If your teacher keeps two sets of records, be sure to go over both with him, as an error may have crept in when the grades were being transferred from one set to another. A surprising number of apparent disagreements will get ironed out right here.

If your teacher balks at this record-checking, explain politely that you want to be sure you and he or she are working from the same basic facts. *You have the right to ask any instructor or TA to check his or her records for accuracy.* Any reasonable teacher should comply with this request. But if your instructor still refuses, it may be best to speak to the head of the teacher's department.

Check also to be sure that the course grade on the grade report your teacher turned in to the registrar's office matches the grade on your report card, since someone in the registrar's office could have erred.

If everything checks out so far, politely ask your instructor what method or formula he or she used to arrive at course grades for class members. Then, together, you and he or she should apply this formula to the grades on your papers, tests, and exams, going step by step through it and arriving at a final grade for the course. Here, too, a surprising number of disputes may be cleared up: sometimes a formula may have been misapplied, or your teacher may have made a simple arithmetic error. (Be sure, of course, that you understand and follow every step of the formula or method, and be sure that it is being properly applied at each step.)

If you and your teacher's records match, and if the method for determining your grade is applied again and yields the same course grade, then you have two options: (1) accept the grade, or (2) argue the merits of the method or formula for determining your final course grade. If your teacher takes into account such intangibles as class participation, and if you feel his or her evaluation of you in such an area is unfair, then you may also wish to argue the merits of that evaluation.

Before I go on, let me make clear that the teacher's method or formula need not be entirely or even partly quantitative. It is the teacher's right—at least in an arts or humanities course—to use as major determinants his or her intuition, observation, and best overall judgment.

If you really don't see anything wrong with your instructor's method of determining course grades, or with any of the grades you have been given throughout the course for your performance, then you should graciously accept the grade you have been given, and go away sadly but politely. But if you do feel that the method for arriving at final course grades is unfair or inappropriate, explain calmly what you feel is wrong with it. You may feel it is an inappropriate way to evaluate everyone's work in that class, or you may feel that it is inappropriate for evaluating your work in particular.

If you object to one or more of the grades you have received on particular tests, exams, papers, and so on, there is nothing wrong with bringing this up.

But it is far better and will have much better results if you bring up these objections very soon after receiving the grades in question. If you bring up the matter weeks later, you will look like you are grasping at straws.

If you ever disagree with or have questions about the grade on an individual paper, test, or exam, make an appointment to see your instructor immediately.

Here's the procedure to follow if the grade on a paper, test, or exam seems wrong or unfair to you.

Make an appointment to meet with your instructor or TA; be decently dressed, on time, and polite. Make sure your grade matches the grade in all your teacher's records; then go through the process of determining that grade with your teacher. Make sure that all answers that have been marked wrong *are* wrong and that all that have been marked correct are correct and have been awarded proper credit. Find out what the grading scale is, and be sure you have been given the proper number of points and the proper grade for that number of points. Then, if necessary and appropriate, discuss the method of grading, the grading scale, or the merits of any of your particular answers or points that have not been looked upon favorably by your instructor.

I recommend against pleading with teachers or telling them things such as "but my parents will kill me if they see this grade." This is humiliating for you and embarrassing for your teacher.

Let's say you have followed all the steps discussed thus far and you still genuinely feel that your grade (either in the course or on a particular paper or test) is unfair, but your instructor still refuses to change it. At this point—but not before—you may bring your case to the head of the teacher's department. Explain what took place in your meeting with your teacher and why you continue to feel your grade is inappropriate or unfair. If your instructor was impolite to you or did not listen to you, or if he or she otherwise treated you badly, explain this, too.

If the head of the department upholds your teacher's decision and you still feel *strongly* that both these people are in the wrong, then you can take your case to the dean of your college, or, in smaller schools, to the dean of academic affairs.

Needless to say, you are going to have to be able to articulate clearly why you feel any grade is unfair or inappropriate. Statements such as "it just seems unfair to me" are not going to get you very far.

Important: do *not* try to get a grade changed just because you wish it were higher. If you are given a grade you feel is deserved, it is both foolish and sleazy to try to get it raised.

Remember, too, that grades are not that big a deal, especially during your freshman and sophomore years. So keep grades in perspective.

A grade of C indicates nothing less than mastery of the course material and a completely acceptable (though average) level of work. A grade of B, despite grade inflation, indicates good work and a mastery of the material that is more than adequate. A grade of B is worth being proud of. A grade of A indicates superior work and an unusu-

ally strong mastery of the material. An A does not indicate merely that you have made no (or few) mistakes, or that you have merely done all that is expected of you, or that the work is simply satisfactory. Only a grade of D, E, or F indicates less than satisfactory work.

I have seen too many students who think an A is barely good enough, and far too many who think they deserve an A just because they "did all the work." The first group should keep in mind that it is humanly impossible to do better than an A, and both groups should remember that an A is reserved, and always has been reserved, for the very top students with unusual skill, talent, or achievement.

The grade of B is also misunderstood. It is looked down upon by parents and students alike, perhaps because we are all used to eating grade A eggs. But a B means "good work," nothing more or less. To complain that a B is substandard because it is not an A is to insult the person who earned that B through his or her sincere effort, and to ignore that very real effort.

A grade of C, while not something to expect praise for, is in all ways utterly respectable. A student who earns all C's in college is going to graduate just like any other student who does acceptable (or better) work. A grade of C is definitely not a mark of distinction, but neither is it a mark of disgrace.

Avoid Incompletes.

An Incomplete is essentially an extension of the deadline by which all the work for a particular class must be completed and turned in. Different schools establish different limits for such extensions. Teachers usually have the prerogative to shorten this deadline as they see fit. Teachers also have the power to refuse to give Incompletes.

If you are having trouble keeping up with one or more of your classes, an Incomplete may seem like an ideal solution: you can postpone some of the work for one course, enabling you to complete more easily the work for the others. Then, when you complete the postponed work later, you still have the chance to earn a high grade in that course.

In theory this works great. In practice, however, it fails as often as it works. The problem here is with the word "postponed." The work is not avoided, merely put off to some future date. Most students think they will be able to find the time later; others tell themselves that they will have to *make* the time; still others have no ability to see into the future, and they unconsciously equate postponing something with never having to deal with it.

Imagine this scenario: you take four courses during the fall term but find you're having trouble keeping up. So you arrange to take an Incomplete in one course. Next term you take four courses again. Now you've got to complete them all, plus part of the class left over from last term. Pretty soon you're in over your head. You couldn't handle four classes last term, and now you've got four and a half . . .

If you do decide to take an Incomplete, be sure to plan in advance how and when you will reasonably be able to make up that work. Be realistic. You may be better off dropping a class than taking an Incomplete in it. The biggest danger of an Incomplete is that once you have opted for it, you have waived your right to drop the course—which means you *must* complete it or take an F.

Two last words on Incompletes: some schools will establish a limit—say, one term—for an Incomplete, but will let you extend it for an additional term with the permission of the instructor. There's nothing wrong with taking a further extension, but remember that you are still only postponing the work, not actually getting any of it done. Remember, too, that your teacher may refuse to extend your Incomplete, even if your school's rules allow him or her to.

Some schools limit the number of Incompletes you may take during any one term, or during your entire college career. Before you take an Incomplete, be sure to check with your registrar to learn your school's regulations on this.

Feel free to use the pass/fail grading option. It can be of great benefit to you.

Pass/fail courses allow you to explore new interests without risking your grade point average. If, for example, you are a mathematics major and you want to take a creative writing course, it's great to be able to take the class without the pressure of grades.

Check your school's regulations regarding pass/fail carefully. Some schools limit the number of credits or courses you may take in pass/fail during any term; others limit the total number of pass/fail credits you may apply toward your degree, or toward completing your major.

Some schools offer the pass/no entry option. This is similar to pass/fail, but in cases where your work is below a certain level (usually below a C−), no entry is made on your transcript. In short, it will be as if you never took the course. My advice regarding pass/fail under this heading and the one that follows applies equally to pass/no entry grading. (Some schools also offer the "no entry" option with letter grades—that is, if you do C− or better work, a letter grade appears on your transcript; if you do worse than C− work, nothing appears on your transcript at all. If a "no entry" option is available to you, either with or without letter grades, I urge you to make use of it.)

Taking some ungraded or pass/fail classes will not hurt your chances of getting into a graduate, professional, or medical school, or of getting a fellowship or scholarship.

Pass/fail courses are not normally computed into your grade point average. As long as you have enough graded courses to compute a GPA that is representative of your ability and achievement as a student, taking pass/fail courses is generally no problem. But there are some tips to be followed:

■ Limit yourself to a very few pass/fail courses in your major department; in your junior and senior years, it is best to take all your courses in your major for letter grades.
■ Take most of your pass/fail courses during your freshman and sophomore years.
■ It is preferable to take introductory courses pass/fail and more ad-

vanced courses for letter grades. (Taking both introductory and advanced classes for letter grades is of course fine also.)

■ As a rule, the farther from your main interests a particular course is, the better off you are taking it in pass/fail, and the less this will bother admissions and selection committees.

■ You can take up to one quarter of your college credits in pass/fail, provided you follow the guidelines I've given, and provided you follow your school's own rules, without its adversely affecting your chances for fellowships, scholarships, and admission to graduate or professional schools.

There are two special guidelines for pre-med students:

■ Pre-meds should be more sparing in their use of the pass/fail option. If you are pre-med, I suggest taking no more than one quarter of your credits in pass/fail.

■ Pre-meds should take *all* of their physical science courses (even Physics, Astronomy, or Plate Tectonics) for letter grades.

If your school offers *only* the pass/fail or pass/no entry option for all its courses, or if it offers written evaluations in place of grades, then of course these limitations do not apply. Graduate, professional, and medical schools, and scholarship and fellowship programs, do not look down on students who have taken pass/fail courses when no other options are available to them. However, I suggest strongly that if you apply to a graduate, professional, or medical school, or to a fellowship or scholarship program, you submit some of your written evaluations as part of your application. These can be evaluations for all the courses in your major; or for all the courses (either in your major or in general) you completed during your junior and senior years; or for all the courses you have taken in college thus far. Choose whichever group makes you look best.

Taking many (or even all) pass/fail courses will almost never hurt your chances of getting a job in your field.

Since employers will never ask about your grades, they are not going to find out that you took a lot of courses in pass/fail. And if, for some reason, a potential employer does ask about your grades, it is very unlikely that the pass/fail classes will bother him or her at all.

It is all right to fail an assignment or even a class once in a while.

No one does well all the time, or should be expected to. If you have done well in everything so far, you are in for some rude shocks in the years to come. Rest assured that you will fail in some things eventually.

Of course, try to do your best and avoid failure whenever possible. But if you blow it once in a while, there's no need to despair or hate yourself.

The key words here are "once in a while." If you generally do fairly well, an occasional screw-up is not a disaster. But if failure is a common occurrence for you, something is wrong. Read the section in Chapter 9 called "Flunking Out," and all of Chapter 10.

Never trade, or offer to trade, sexual favors for credits or grades.

Students make such offers to teachers more often than people think, and more often than teachers or administrators publicly admit. The same is true of teachers offering good grades in exchange for sex.

I strongly advise against making such offers to teachers, not only because it's sleazy, but also because it can have effects that are much more far-reaching than you had intended. What began as a simple little business deal between you and the instructor can turn into the ruin of a marriage, the splitting up of a family, or the destruction of a promising teaching career. Such melodramatic scenarios have in fact happened, all because a student offered to trade sex for a good grade.

And if a teacher approaches *you* with the offer of a high grade in exchange for sex, report him or her to your dean immediately. Don't let the teacher intimidate you, and don't worry about harming his or her career. The teacher is violating one of the most basic ethical principles in teaching and in education, and his or her superiors should know about it.

Important: a teacher making an unwanted pass at you, either politely or crudely, is a *very* different thing from him or her offering to trade a good grade for sex. A teacher who wants to make the grade-sex trade is compromising his or her role as teacher as well as your role as student. But a simple pass or attempted seduction exists outside the student-teacher realm. See Chapter 5 for a detailed discussion of this topic.

Teachers and Staff

Teachers and administrators, like members of every other profession, range from excellent to terrible.

A good teacher should be interesting, interested in his or her subject, sensitive to the needs of each class and each student, able to communicate clearly and precisely to his or her students, accessible and available on a regular basis, and generally warmhearted and pleased with his or her job.

Perhaps one of three college teachers meets these standards, so choose your teachers with great care. Many, perhaps most, teachers are only passably interesting—and a fair number are outright dull or confusing.

Chapter 3 discusses in detail how to locate the best instructors.

Never judge a teacher by his or her rank, or by how well known or well praised that teacher may be by the academic community, or by how long he or she has been teaching. None of this information will tell you how good or poor an instructor this person is; you will have to find this out for yourself.

Absurd as it may seem, most college

teachers are hired and given tenure not for their teaching ability but because of their research, publications, or status in their fields. Their ability and performance as teachers are largely or entirely ignored by many administrators and committees.

Even intelligence and wisdom do not necessarily correlate with good teaching. Some of the most brilliant and famous thinkers in academia are rotten teachers. The worst teacher I ever had in college was known as a brilliant scholar, had substantial publications, and was head of his department.

Remember, though, that teachers and administrators make mistakes, just like everybody else, and they suffer from normal human failures and weaknesses. So don't put them on pedestals or expect them to be perfect, because they aren't. And don't condemn them for *occasional* mistakes or poor judgment.

Avoid taking classes taught by boring, incompetent, pompous, or obnoxious teachers under all but the most desperate or unavoidable circumstances.

If you do take one of these classes, the chances are good that you will be bored or confused, that you will dislike the class, and that you will learn little. The chances are also excellent that you will not get a very good grade. So why make things difficult for yourself? Head off this problem at the pass by avoiding the poor teachers.

Although most teachers are knowledgeable or expert in their fields, this does not necessarily mean that they are

*particularly knowledgeable about any-
thing else, even if they think and say
they are.*

Some teachers, particularly those
who are well known in their particular
fields, presume their wisdom extends
into other areas. Sometimes it really *does*
encompass other subjects, but often it
does not. Beware of teachers who try to
shove their bogus "wisdom" down your
throat. And beware of those who simply
expect you to accept whatever they
might say about other subjects on faith.

Some teachers, sadly, get elevated
to guru status. But no matter how re-
vered or respected these teachers may
be, don't let your own good judgment
be swept away by their charisma, or by
the adulation they receive from others.

You are going to have to make your
own judgments about the correctness,
reliability, authenticity, or wisdom of
each statement each of your teachers
makes. The ability to make these judgments yourself is one of the best things
college can teach you. You are going to
learn this the hard way—by hearing
respected people spouting bullshit; by
learning exactly contradictory things
from two different teachers, each of
whom insists the other is off his rocker;
and perhaps by disagreeing and even
arguing with some of your instructors.

Remember, teachers—just like
other people—may be biased, closed-
minded, or just plain wrong about certain things, even in their own fields.
Many of these teachers will emphatically
or furiously deny their own bias or
ignorance.

Some teachers are not even terribly
knowledgeable about the subjects they
are teaching. (This is much more com-

mon than most students suspect.) Some teachers will present their opinions as facts; others will present falsehoods as facts. Some will belabor the obvious; others will attempt to refute the obvious.

Take with a grain of salt everything a teacher or textbook says, and examine critically everything you learn. This skill will prove enormously valuable to you in the future.

It is all right to disagree with a teacher or to have different beliefs about a topic or a situation, or to feel that he or she is wrong about something.

Don't let a teacher force a belief or opinion down your throat. This does not mean you have to argue every time you disagree. But *never* think, "Oh, what do I know? I'm only a student and she's a teacher" or "He's got a Ph.D. and ten years of teaching experience, so he must be right." And never let yourself be intimidated by a teacher who uses such an argument against you. If you do wish to argue a point with a teacher, either in or out of class, feel free to do so *politely* and calmly. However, do not become visibly upset, and do not resort to personal attacks on the teacher. You are not likely to change a teacher's mind, though this does happen sometimes. But the point of a discussion or an argument is not merely to express your point of view, or to try to win your teacher over. You may find that your teacher's point of view is one you have never thought of or understood before, and thus the discussion or argument may be beneficial to you, whether or not it actually alters your opinion. It may be beneficial to your teacher, too, for the same reason.

If you are arguing in class, be fair to the other students and don't take up too much of the class's time. After a few minutes, shelve the argument; if you like, bring it up privately with the instructor after class.

Teachers hold little real power over a student.

Many students are afraid of disagreeing or arguing with a teacher because of possible repercussions. Often these repercussions are more imagined than real.

A teacher has the power to hurt you in the following ways—and *only* in these ways:

1. He or she can give you a poor grade.

2. He or she can write a poor recommendation on your behalf (in this case, a "recommendation" that does not recommend you at all); or he or she can refuse to write a recommendation for you. However, if you are having trouble with a teacher, chances are you wouldn't want a recommendation from him or her anyway.

3. The teacher can bad-mouth you to his or her colleagues, and to others he or she knows. This is unlikely to do you much harm unless you are an undergraduate and plan to continue with graduate work in the same department at the same school. Even then it may not make a difference, depending on how much weight your teacher's word carries with his or her colleagues.

* * *

In general, teachers and administrators are fair and decent people. If you feel you *have* been treated unfairly by a teacher or administrator, however, feel free to take your problem to that person's superior.

Never be afraid of a teacher or an administrator, and never let one intimidate you.

Most college teachers and administrators are friendly, even solicitous. However, a few teachers and administrators like to feel powerful and in control. If you do find yourself threatened or intimidated, be polite but assert your own rights, and don't let the teacher or administrator frighten you. If you feel it is appropriate, bring the matter to that person's superior. Explain how and why you were threatened or intimidated.

Teaching Assistants (TA's) often are new to teaching, and often they make mistakes.

Sometimes TA's, even those new to teaching, are among the best teachers.

But many TA's are awkward teachers. Some are ignorant or inept. On the average, TA's tend to be slightly poorer teachers than regular faculty. This does not mean you should avoid TA's. Follow the instructions in Chapter 3 in choosing a TA. Be particularly careful in making your choice. But give TA's some slack. They need and deserve it. They'll make mistakes; let some of these, though not serious or repeated ones, go by. And take everything a TA says and does with one extra grain of salt.

Always feel free to ask your teacher or TA for help when you need it. Likewise, feel free to ask any teacher any question, no matter how elementary it may seem.

Teachers are walking resources of information and ideas. They are paid not merely to teach classes but also to be available to students who need their help.

If you are having trouble with one of your classes, or if there is something you do not understand, go to your teacher or TA. There is nothing wrong with this at all, and your teacher will not look down on you or think you are a dull-witted or inferior person. Explain what you are having trouble with, and ask for his or her assistance. If you need to do this on a regular basis, that's perfectly fine.

These private conferences with teachers can be enormously helpful. Often an instructor can make something clear to you in only a couple of minutes of private conversation, even if hours of lecture by the same teacher have left you in the dark.

If a teacher refuses to give you help when you need it, or if he or she takes the attitude of "if you can't do it without my help, that's your problem and your tough luck," he or she is shirking a primary responsibility as a teacher. I'd go to another teacher in the same department for help.

You do not have to be in a teacher's class to ask for advice, help, or guidance.

The minute you register as a student, every teacher in your school is at

your disposal. It doesn't matter whether
you need information for a class, for a
paper you are writing, or just to satisfy
your own curiosity. Ask—it's your priv-
ilege as a student.

This is especially helpful if the information you seek is elementary, or if it
is something you "should" have learned
in high school. After all, if you don't ask,
you still won't know. If you're too embarrassed to ask one of your own teachers about something so simple, ask a
teacher who doesn't know you. Use the
telephone if you're ashamed to ask in
person. The longer your embarrass-
ment keeps you from asking, the longer
you won't know the answer—but once
you've asked, you'll get the answer, and
you won't need to feel embarrassed
anymore.

Some teachers are at their best in front of a class. Others are strongest one-to-one.

I know some teachers who give
terrific lectures and who are great at
leading discussions, but in private con-
versations they are dull and not very
helpful. Others are interesting and in-
spiring on a one-to-one basis, but in
class they are academic cold fish.

So don't count out a teacher entirely if he or she is a bore in the classroom.
You may find that the same teacher will
be ideal to work with on an independent
study project. The opposite of this is
equally true.

Be on time for appointments with teachers and other college personnel.

This can make a much bigger difference than you might think. If you are

prompt and reliable, teachers and administrators are apt to think more highly of you, and they are likely to be more cooperative and to treat you with more courtesy and respect. The same is true for dressing neatly and being polite. I don't mean wearing suits and saying "sir" and "ma'am," but simply looking decent and acting presentably and pleasantly. The small amount of effort this takes can make a large difference in the way teachers and administrators treat you and think of you. It shouldn't really make such a difference—but sometimes it does.

This certainly holds true in the outside world, too, especially among prospective employers. (Note: a job interview is one of the few situations where you *should* dress better than just "presentably.")

One final word on being on time: teachers and administrators are notorious for being late for appointments, for failing to show up for appointments or meetings at all, and for ignoring their own posted office hours. Because this is so common, and because teachers seem so unrepentant about it, your best bet is to establish a double standard: always be on time yourself, but never get angry if your teacher shows up late, or fails to show up at all. (Of course, if he or she doesn't show, be sure to leave a note saying you were there and asking to make a new appointment.)

Do not play up to teachers.

For one thing, this is sleazy and dishonest. You are simply trying to trade compliments, attention, or gifts for a good grade.

Usually this ploy doesn't work at all,

since your teacher will almost certainly see through it quickly unless he or she is unusually vain.

The big problem with playing up to teachers is that it may backfire. Some teachers are annoyed by students who try to charm or manipulate them.

A bigger, though somewhat less likely, danger is that a teacher may take your praise and attention as an expression of your romantic interest in him or her. If he or she tries to return this perceived interest, you will suddenly find yourself in very deep water.

Don't think you will automatically avoid this problem if your instructor is the same sex as you. There are quite a few closet gay and bisexual people teaching college. Your teacher may just assume you learned of his or her sexual preferences through the gay grapevine. Needless to say, such a misunderstanding could put you in *very* deep water.

This doesn't mean you shouldn't try to be friends with a teacher you like. If your interest is genuinely friendly, feel free to invite any of your teachers to a party, to lunch, to a movie, or whatever. Friendships between students and teachers are quite common, and sometimes they last a long time. But don't fake an interest in a teacher for the sake of your own personal advancement.

If you don't like your adviser, or if you don't like his or her advice, you can and probably should seek a new adviser.

In most schools, you can choose any teacher you wish for your adviser, provided the teacher agrees to take on that role. Some schools will arbitrarily assign you an adviser when you first enroll.

But you need not stick with the adviser you have been assigned. And in most schools, you can change advisers for any reason at just about any time, though you may need to notify your registrar and/or your major department in writing of this change. (Note: in some schools your adviser must teach in your major department, and in some schools or programs you may need your adviser's approval to graduate.)

If your adviser is obnoxious, thoughtless, or less than helpful, of course seek a new adviser. But feel free to change advisers for any other reason. For example, you may simply not feel especially comfortable with your current adviser, even though he or she is a good teacher and a decent human being. Or you may want someone whose educational philosophies or interests are closer to your own.

An adviser's job is to help you reach your own educational goals, and to help you become a thinking, compassionate, and well-educated person. Therefore, you should listen carefully to your adviser's advice and suggestions. But if, after careful consideration, you disagree with your adviser, you will probably be best off if you find a different adviser, one who is more generally supportive of your goals and interests. After all, you want an adviser who will be on your side, not someone you will wind up arguing with.

There is nothing inherently wrong or unethical about having a romance with a teacher. However, such a romance will have all the same possibilities and potential problems as a romance with a non-teacher.

I know of several such romances that have worked out well, and, of course, of several that have not.

If you begin a romantic relationship with a teacher, remember that he or she has strengths, weaknesses, and neuroses, just like everyone else. If you are attracted to a teacher because he or she seems unusually wise, competent, compassionate, or generally wonderful, you are going to find out in the course of your relationship how that person is less than perfect. When this happens, don't condemn the teacher for turning out to be human after all. He or she was human all along.

Do not get involved (or even flirt) with a teacher or other staff member who is married, engaged, or otherwise "taken."

This person has a career and a relationship going already. An outside affair could harm his or her career, break up his or her home, or have some other disastrous result. What may have seemed to you like a simple fling or affair may in fact have large and far-ranging consequences. So consider these potential consequences very carefully *before* you express your romantic interest.

If a teacher makes an unwanted pass at you, turn it down firmly but politely. If the teacher persists, ask him or her to stop. If he or she still persists, talk to the dean.

There is nothing wrong with a teacher flirting with you or making a pass at you. After all, you are both adults, and adults flirt and make passes at one another all the time. There *is* something wrong, however, with a teacher making passes at you *once you have made it clear that you aren't interested in him or her*. Be sure your turn-down is completely straightforward and clear, and not open to misinterpretation as uncertainty, seductiveness, coyness, or whatnot.

If the teacher threatens retribution (usually a low grade) in return for your refusal to get romantically involved, or if he or she offers you a high grade in exchange for sex, this man or woman should not be teaching. Go to your dean at once and explain exactly what happened.

If you have a grievance with a teacher or other staff member, first try to work things out directly with that person. Be both assertive and polite. If this does not work, speak to the head of that teacher's department. If this fails to resolve the problem, see your dean.

When problems arise, try to deal with them promptly. Don't wait until the problem has escalated into something much larger, or until it has been totally forgotten by the teacher.

Make an appointment to talk with the teacher or TA in his or her office. Explain what you feel the problem is. Be honest, direct, and straightforward. Let the teacher or TA respond to your complaint before continuing the discussion yourself.

No matter what happens, try to keep calm, and be polite. Don't get visibly angry or hysterical, and don't resort to pleading, whining, tears, or insults. But do be straightforward and assertive.

If you are having problems with a TA who assists a regular instructor or professor with a class, and your discussion with the TA fails to resolve the problem, speak to the instructor of that class.

CHAPTER 6

Papers, Tests, and Exams

A college paper states a specific point, then documents that point through argument and evidence.

This is the primary rule for most college papers in virtually every subject. Once you have grasped it, writing papers should come much more easily to you.

It doesn't matter whether you outline your papers before starting to write, or whether you just write draft after draft until everything comes together, or whether you sit down, start writing, and turn out something clear and precise off the top of your head. Use whatever method works best for you. You may need to use different methods for different papers. Sometimes a combination of methods works.

But no matter what method or methods you use, the final paper you hand in should begin by stating a specific point (also called a thesis or thesis statement). It should then prove that point, step by step.

A point is a complete statement that can be argued. "The causes of the

American revolution" is not a point; it is merely a topic. "The Revolutionary War was caused primarily by British intolerance" *is* a point, however. "The Revolutionary War was caused primarily by British intolerance and secondarily by American hotheadedness; British ignorance was not a major cause, however" is also a point, but a much more complex one. The first point might be appropriate for a five-page paper, the second for a fifteen-page paper.

"Fitzgerald and Faulkner are similar in some ways and different in others" is not a point, because any two things in the universe are similar in some ways and different in others. "Fitzgerald and Faulkner both wrote about America and some of its more desperate characters" *is* a point, but one that is so obvious that it doesn't really deserve mentioning, let alone arguing. "Fitzgerald and Faulkner both wrote about America and Americans in their short stories, but Faulkner delved deeper into the American heart" *would* be a good point for a paper.

Your point should be clear, yet not so self-evident that your paper seems simplistic or obvious. Everything in your paper should support that point; if it doesn't, get rid of it. The idea is to make the tightest, most convincing argument for your point that you can.

In a college paper or essay test, deal with one topic, idea, or concept at a time.

This is the second most important rule for almost all college writing. Your paper will be clearest and most convincing if you prove your point one item or step at a time. Once you start writing about a topic—for instance, Melville's adventures in the South Seas—do *not* start writing about anything else until you've finished with Melville in the South Seas. Then move on to the next topic, perhaps Melville in Honolulu.

Whenever you change your focus, perspective, topic, train of thought, or approach, begin a new paragraph.

Keep your focus narrow and specific, both in papers and on tests.

The more general you are, the more words you are going to need to support your point, and the more difficult writing is going to be for you. Many students have trouble with papers simply because they choose focuses that are too broad.

For example, if your point is "Cities in Europe are less prone to urban decline than cities in America," you are going to need at least fifty pages to make a decent argument that this is so. "German cities are less prone to urban decline than American cities with large German populations" is still rather general and would probably take twenty-five or thirty pages. But the following point could likely be well argued in fifteen pages: "Milwaukee and Bonn are both major industrial cities, but the attitudes of the people of Bonn make it a city that is surprisingly resilient to urban decline, while the attitudes of Milwaukee's populace make it much more vulnerable to this decline." (I don't know the first thing about Milwaukee or Bonn; I'm picking them at random for the purpose of this explanation.)

In the first example, you would have to deal with the history and sociology of two continents; in the second, you would still need to look at what makes two entire countries tick. But in the third, you need only focus on selected attitudes of the inhabitants of two cities.

Connecting ideas and making the transition from one idea to another are crucial writing skills.

Transitions and connections give a great many students problems. Following two general rules should solve this problem for you in most cases:

1. When you change focus, perspective, topic, or train of thought, provide your reader with a transition. In many cases, this can be as simple as "On the other hand," or "In contrast," or "Similarly," or "_____ is another good example of this phenomenon."

In some cases, though, the connection may not be so obvious or the transition so easy to make. You may need an entire paragraph to make a connection or transition. This should be as complex and as explanatory as necessary, but at the same time as short, clear, and simple as possible.

2. Transitions and connections can be made with *any* unifying factor. For example, if you need to make the transition between cuckoo clocks and strawberry ice cream, you might write, "There is something homey and comforting about the sight of a cuckoo leaping out of his mechanical home and announcing the time. For my money, though, I prefer the more sensual pleasures—like music or strawberry ice cream."

If you can't figure out how to make

a connection or transition, *make up* a unifying factor. Almost anything will do, even a unifying word. For example, suppose you are stuck making the transition between the IRT subway line and Lady Godiva's bare breasts—about the most difficult example I can come up with. You might write something like this: "If you've been in New York recently, you know that the residents of that city have been making a lot of noise about the poor service the IRT has been providing. But I believe the public furor is destined to die down. A few centuries back, the residents of another city made plenty of noise when Lady Godiva rode naked through the streets on a horse— but a few weeks after that incident, Ms. Godiva was nothing more than a source of entertaining gossip. Soon even that died down: there is only so much you can say about one's exposed bosom." (The unifying factor here is the word and concept *noise*.)

The ability to sound knowledgeable and to be convincing is as important, and sometimes more important, than what you actually know about the subject.

Of course, the more you know about what you are discussing, the better. But on a test or in a paper, don't let on that you are lacking in knowledge or awareness. If you can't remember the year the Wright Brothers flew at Kitty Hawk, don't say, "When the Wright Brothers made their famous flight sometime around 1915 . . ." Instead write, "When the Wright Brothers made their famous flight early in our century . . ." If you aren't sure whether flies or bees communicate with one another by dancing, say, "We have known for some time that certain insect species speak to one another through a dance."

And *never* bring in any information that might undermine your point or any of your arguments. If, for example, you want to argue that George Washington was a model president, don't mention that he kept slaves and had illegitimate children.

Do not try to sound scholarly or academic on tests or in papers. All writing should be as clear, as direct, and as concise as possible.

This bit of information surprises, even shocks, some students when they first get to college. But two of the first things some college students have to *unlearn* are convoluted language and unnecessary jargon. Don't say "Berg asserts that members of the female sex have a tendency to enjoy a longer life-span than their male counterparts," when you can say, "According to Berg, women live longer than men."

Some high school English teachers teach their students to write in this convoluted and high-falutin' style and reward them for doing it. Also, a good many academicians and a great many executives, bureaucrats, and political speechwriters misuse the English language in this same way. But it is still misuse. If what you want to say is "But it seems to me that Berg is missing the point," say it just like that.

There is one exception to this general rule. Although you should avoid using all unnecessary jargon, you *should* use jargon when it is clearly required by your teacher or your field of study. The fields of urban planning, education, and social work frequently make heavy use of jargon, and you may be expected to use it yourself. The jargon is no more appropriate or necessary from a linguistic point of view, but its use may be necessary for your academic survival. To a lesser degree, this applies to many other areas of the social sciences.

Most successful college papers end with a concluding paragraph (or group of paragraphs) that add to the point of the paper without merely restating it.

Once you have proven your point, you need a few sentences that give a feeling of completeness and conclusion to your paper. This is more stylistic than anything else, but it is nonetheless important, at least in terms of sounding convincing and pleasing your teacher.

It is *not* enough merely to restate your point—that is mere redundance. You must add a twist or nuance.

For example, if you have just written a paper on why mass transportation will never become more popular in American cities, you might end with: "While it might seem ultimately in our best interests to be more sympathetic to mass transit, we must remember that sympathy and practicality are very different animals. I can be sympathetic to the unemployed, but that does not mean I should quit my job so that someone else can have it. Despite the benefits that mass transit can provide, and despite my own desire that there be more buses and fewer cars on the road, I am not about to give up my own automobile for the sake of the public good. From my own point of view, that would be quite impractical indeed."

Teachers will not always tell you what they want in a paper. Sometimes they do not even know what they want themselves.

Far too many teachers, especially those in the humanities, give assignments such as "Write a ten-page paper on one of Shaw's plays." This is not much to go on; all you know are your general subject and the required length. This is fine if you know exactly what you want to write; but many students want or need more guidance.

Many teachers who give vague writing assignments have a fairly clear idea of what they want or expect from students, but they are unwilling or unable to articulate it.

If you are given an assignment you feel is too vague, feel free to ask the teacher to clarify it; or, ask if he or she has any particular approaches or themes to suggest. Sometimes this will net you a clarification or explanation. Often, however, it will not; you'll get a response such as, "I'd rather leave that up to you." You will have to live with this response, I'm afraid.

One option you have at this point is to think of several possible thesis statements for papers, then call or visit your instructor and run the topics by him or her. He or she can then approve, disapprove, or otherwise react to your ideas. Such a discussion may also provide useful clarification of your own ideas, and/or more of an idea of what your teacher is looking for. You may even want to run the general argument of your paper by your teacher orally. His or her comments at this point may prove extremely useful, and they may help you write a better, tighter, and sounder paper.

Be responsive to the question or the assignment. If this is impossible, sound as though you are being responsive to the question or the assignment.

If you are given the essay question, "Discuss the role of Buddhism in the thought of Eric Fromm," don't mess with Hinduism or Freud. Deal with the subject as straightforwardly as you can. Don't digress unless your digression supports your point, and even then get back to your main subject as quickly as you can.

If you are short on knowledge, write your answer or paper as if you knew everything you needed to know—that is, keep your form the same, include what information you can, and sound authoritative about what you do know.

When you finish writing a paper or an answer to an essay question, check it to make sure everything you have written supports your point and is responsive to that question or assignment.

The papers teachers like best are both interesting and responsive to the assignment. It is proper and sometimes even recommended to be original and creative in college papers, provided they are responsive to the assignment.

For most teachers, reading papers is a disagreeable chore. Most college papers are deadly dull.

But if you can liven up your own paper so it is entertaining, you will please and very possibly delight your teacher.

This doesn't mean forsaking content for entertainment. Your paper should fulfill all the requirements of the assignment. Don't go overboard; don't try to be *too* cute or clever for your own good. But if your paper makes some good points and is fun to read as well, you are sitting pretty.

With some thought you can probably come up with several interesting formats on your own. Here are a few that have been used (and that have done well) in the past:

■ Do a self-interview, in which you ask yourself questions and respond to them in the standard interview format.
■ Illustrate an otherwise serious paper with James Thurber-like illustrations and captions. For example, if you are discussing Faulkner's incessant rewriting of *The Sound and the Fury*, you might draw on a separate page a picture of a harried-looking man scribbling furiously. He is surrounded by hundreds of manuscripts titled "Draft 808," "Draft 955," etc. The caption: "William was having trouble sleeping."
■ Write a short playlet in which the characters discuss and act out the points you have to make.

These points apply only to papers, not to essay exams. On exams, you should be as precise and straightforward as possible.

It is a good idea to type all your papers or have someone else type them, even if your instructor will accept handwritten papers.

In general, teachers respond slightly better to typewritten papers than they do to handwritten ones. You will also be doing a service to your instructors, whose eyes will doubtless be tired from reading all those other handwritten papers.

If you cannot type, hire a typist. Your school newspaper should have several ads for typists in its classified section, and almost any college bulletin board will have plenty of ads for typists posted. The going rate for typing is $1.00 to $1.25 per double-spaced page. (All papers should be double-spaced, though footnotes and quotes may be single-spaced.)

Always proofread any exam or paper carefully before turning it in.

You want every paper and exam to be in the best possible shape, so don't overlook the fine points. Make sure every word is spelled correctly; if you're not sure of the proper spelling, look it up. Also be sure that all your grammar and punctuation are proper. If you are unsure of any of this, ask someone who *is* sure.

The better a paper or essay looks, the more positively your teacher will react. And some teachers, petty as it may seem, penalize students for errors in grammar, punctuation, or spelling. Obviously, you do not want to receive a failing grade for an otherwise excellent paper because you consistently misspelled the word "cemetery." (English teachers are not the only ones who levy these penalties. There are people who teach history, geology, and sociology who expect letter-perfect papers from their students, and who do things like lower grades for misspelled words and improper grammar. This is pretty rare—perhaps one teacher out of twenty engages in such practices—but don't be too shocked if you wind up with such a teacher.)

If someone else types your papers for you, you should still proofread each page. Many typists are not especially good proofreaders, and you do not want to be blamed for errors your typist made.

Always keep a copy of every paper you hand in.

Teachers lose papers occasionally, and there is always the chance of a freak accident in which the paper disappears or is destroyed. So *always* make a carbon copy or photocopy of each paper before you turn it in. If the paper does disappear, you can simply hand in the copy in its place. But before you hand in the copy, make a copy of it! Though it is very rare, teachers have been known to lose two copies of the same paper.)

Save your copy of each paper until you have received your final grade for the course. There is always the small possibility that your teacher will give you a high grade on a paper, then mistakenly mark in his or her grade book that you turned nothing in, or that you received a lower grade than you actually did receive. If something like this happens, you will be able to bring in a copy of the paper as evidence. Save all your returned and graded papers for this reason.

It really isn't a bad idea to save copies of papers indefinitely. These are useful in the event that potential employers, graduate or professional school admissions committees request a sample of your academic writing, or a sample of your writing in general.

If you do not understand an assignment or question fully, ask the teacher, TA, or exam proctor for clarification.

Don't worry about sounding ignorant or dense. The chances are good that other students are just as confused as you are but are afraid to ask.

A surprisingly large number of teachers are not especially good at formulating clear questions and assignments. So if you are unsure about something, or if it seems unclear, ask. And ask out loud, so that the other students can hear.

Most schools have drop-in writing labs open to all students.

Nearly every college has a facility for one-to-one help with your writing. Usually this is called a writing lab, writing center, or writing clinic. It may be staffed by regular instructors, by graduate and/or undergraduate students, by writing specialists, or by some combination of these.

If you are having trouble writing one or more of your papers or exams, or if your grades on papers and exams are not as high as you would like, it is probably a good idea to use these labs.

It is perfectly ethical to get assistance from a writing lab or writing tutor for any paper or assignment you have been given. Whether you need help coming up with the basic point for a paper, organizing or outlining a paper, actually writing or rewriting the paper,